A

GRAMMAR

OF THE

RONG (LEPCHA) LANGUAGE

A

GRAMMAR

OF THE

RONG (LEPCHA) LANGUAGE,

AS IT EXISTS IN THE DORJELING AND SIKIM HILLS.

BY

COLONEL G. B. MAINWARING,

BENGAL STAFF CORPS.

GYAN

Published by

Gyan Publishing House
5, Ansari Road
Daryaganj, New Delhi-110002
Phone: 011-47034999, 9811692060
E-mail: books@gyanbooks.com

Distribution Network
gyanbooks.com
India, USA, Canada, UK, Australia

ISBN: 978-81-212-5995-8 (PB)
First Published, 1876

2nd Impression 2024

Printed at: Gyan Press, Delhi.

A GRAMMAR OF THE RONG (LEPCHA) LANGUAGE
Author: G. B. MAINWARING

A GRAMMAR OF THE RONG (LEPCHA) LANGUAGE,

AS IT EXISTS IN THE DORJELING AND SIKIM HILLS.

BY

COLONEL G. B. MAINWARING,

BENGAL STAFF CORPS.

CALCUTTA:

PRINTED BY C. B. LEWIS, BAPTIST MISSION PRESS.

1876.

To

THE HON'BLE E. C. BAYLEY, C. S. I.

Member of the Council of the Governor General of India.

As a slight tribute of respect for his great attainments in Philology and in general knowledge, and for the advancement he renders both personally and by encouragement to all literature and science, this book is gratefully dedicated.

Calcutta, December 1875.

PREFACE AND INTRODUCTORY REMARKS.

Before presenting to the public a grammar of a language, it may be considered meet to give some information regarding the country and people, especially where, as in the present instance, little is known respecting either. Relating to the Lepchas and country, however, little information can be imparted. Sikim is in Lat. 27° 2′ 53″ N. Lon. 88° 18′ 41″ E. and is bounded on the North by Tibet; on the East by Prú (Bútán); on the West by Nepal; and formerly extended on the South to near Titalyah in the Plains.

It was not until the year 1814 that the first political connection with Sikim commenced, and then only with reference to the affairs of Nepal. The first communication of importance with the latter, commenced in 1767, when the reigning Newah Rajah, harassed incessantly by the independent Gúrkhas* who were now threatening his capital (Kathmandah), became alarmed and besought the aid of the British Government in India. It being considered politic to retain in peace the great mercantile and agricultural commerce which existed between Bengal and Nepal, and thence extended, through the latter country, to Tibet and China, his request was acceded to, and a force, under Capt. Kinloch, was sent to his aid, but, unfortunately, the troops despatched were totally inadequate for the occasion. They arrived in Nepal in the commencement of the rains (1767); the malarious and deadly climate of the Terai, and want of provisions soon prostrated the few and unseasoned natives of the Plains, and Kinloch was obliged to retire. The Gúrkhas relieved from unrestraint, did not wait for a second force to be sent, but renewed the attack with unprecedented vigor and shortly took Kathmandah. Wholesale and indiscriminate slaughter ensued, all the ruling Newah chiefs were put to the sword, and midst uncontrolled bloodshed and unheard of atrocities, the Gúrkha chief, Prithwi Narayn, became the ruler of the kingdom. Elated with their success, which added to their hill territories the country of Nepal, comprising the vallies of Tirhút and Sarun,

* The Newahs were the Budhist inhabitants of Nepal. The Gúrkhas were bigoted Hindus: grasping and rapacious, they, at first, gradually, and afterwards rapidly invaded and possessed themselves of the territories of the numerous independent chiefs who held sway in the Himalayas. The conquest of Nepal and of Sikim, united their possessions, making them masters of all the Hill and Terai tract, from the rivers Sutlej in the N. West, to the Rung-nyo (Teistah) in the S. East.

the Gúrkhas aspired to the conquest of Tibet and China.* The former country they invaded, reduced part to subjection and occupied it; but were ignominiously driven out by Chinese troops in 1792. They, however, still held in possession the country of Sikim, which they had subjugated after the conquest of Nepal, and retained in domination by a series of fortified intrenchments and barricades. I am not writing a history of Nepal, it would therefore be foreign to the present subject to recount all the events which succeeded that calamitous triumph of the Gúrkhas, which, for many years, plunged a peaceful, prosperous and most flourishing country into a state of anarchy, into constant civil broils and contentions, and rendered it a scene of ungoverned passions and of appalling barbarities.† It was in vain the British Government intermediated, in vain it strove to keep in check the violence that convulsed the country. Treaties were made but to be broken by Nepal; the British Envoy was treated with duplicity and disrespect. Wearied with the constant discord and reiterated aggressions, the Government of India declared war in 1814;‡

---

* The invasion of Tibet, and pillage of the Grand Lamasery of Degarchhe were also in a great measure due to the influence of a Lama, known as, Samhur, (his true name and title were Sha-kar Khyem-bo; literally, Sha-kar, the learned), brother of the བཀྲ་ཤིས *bkra-shis* (Anglice, Teshi) Lama, who, on the death of the latter, fled from Lhasa. Having brought much plundered treasure with him, he was taken into favor by the Nepal chief. Afterwards, on the peremptory demand of the Chinese authorities for his surrender, to avoid being delivered over, he put an end to his life by poison.

† A graphic account is given of the state of Nepal during this early period by an eye-witness, a Roman Catholic Priest (Father Guiseppe, Prefect to the Roman Mission), who was a resident at Nepal for four years; he states, — to firmly secure the valley of Nepal, the Gúrkha Chief hoped to effect this purpose by causing a famine, that orders for this were issued and vigorously carried into effect——"Every person who "was found on the road carrying even a little salt or cotton was hung on a tree, and he caused all the inha- "bitants of a neighbouring village to be put to death in a most cruel manner, even women and children did "not escape, for having supplied a little cotton to the inhabitants of Nepal; and when I arrived in that "country in the beginning of 1769, it was a most horrible spectacle to behold so many people hanging on trees "in the road."— He relates that the besieged, in a fortress (Khirtapúr), submitted themselves prisoners under a promise of general amnesty, but that after their surrender, Prithwi Narayan sent instructions to his brother, (whom he had placed in possession of the surrounding country), to cut off the lips and noses of every one, and that all these (lips and noses) were to be preserved —"that he might ascertain how many souls there were."—The order was carried into execution with every cruelty and horror, none escaping, (neither women nor children), except the players of wind instruments, who alone were spared. Many in despair put an end to their lives— "it was most shocking to see so many living people with their teeth and noses resembling the skulls of the "deceased." With sarcastic and diabolical jocularity, Prithwi Narayn afterwards changed the name of the town to Naskatpúr, = the place of cut noses. He did not survive long to enjoy what fruits he may have reaped; he died two years after, in 1771.

‡ On the first threat of war by the British, in the early part of the year, the subject was referred, by the Rajah, for the decision of the Chiefs. Though the recommendation of a temporizing and conciliating policy, urged by prudent counsellors, was in the majority, the boast — that the Gúrkhas were invincible and their country impregnable — was paramount. War was determined on. Hostilities were immediately commenced by a force proceeding and slaughtering almost all of the few men that composed our Police outposts of Bhutwal.

and in the latter end of that year a force was sent under command of Sir David Ochterlony. Having overcome the Nepal troops, the latter sued for peace. In framing conditions, one of the stipulations was, that the Gúrkhas should relinquish all claim to the territory, usurped by them, belonging to the Sikim Ruler. They would not accede to all the terms. The campaign was therefore renewed, under the same General. Instructions were also sent to Capt. Latter, the Political Agent on the Eastern Nepal frontier, to render the Sikim king every assistance in his power to expel the Gúrkhas from his territories. Nepal being completely subdued, the treaty of Segowlee, bearing date the 2nd December, 1815, was formally signed and sealed, in which, by the 5th and 6th Articles, the Nepal Government renounced all claim to the land east of the Mechi river, and further bound itself, never to molest the king of Sikim, or invade his territories, that all differences should be referred to the arbitration of the British Government—"by whose award the Rajah of Nepal engages to abide."— It was not, however, until afterwards driven out by a force under Captain Latter, that the Gúrkhas eventually evacuated the Sikim territory.

Sikim was considered of special importance as affording an accessible approach to Eastern Tibet, and, as such, was deemed advantageous to be retained by a friendly power. The following year, therefore, a covenant was entered into by Captain Latter, on the part of the Governor-General Lord Moira, securing, to the king of Sikim, the whole of his territories. This covenant was delivered to the deputies of the king, at Tirhút, on the 10th day of February 1817. For some years after this, nothing of importance took place between the British Government and Sikim. In 1827, disputes, with regard to the boundaries, occurring between Nepal and Sikim, Captain Lloyd, commanding the frontier force at Titalyah, and Mr. J. W. Grant, Commercial Resident at Maldah (who had before visited the hills), were ordered to proceed to Sikim to amicably arrange matters. Both were charmed with the country and the inhabitants (the Lepchas).* They selected the site of Dorjeling,† as a most

---

* I use the term Lepcha; as it has been so long employed, it may be considered to have become Anglicised; I do not know the origin of the word, but it is doubtless a denomination of the Gúrkhas, from whom most of the names of the neighbouring places &c., have been taken, instead of from the inhabitants of the respective countries, *e. g.* Sikim, Butan, Tibet, &c. The proper name of the Lepchas, as they call themselves, is—Róng.

† The Tibetans had before this time formed a settlement at Dorjeling, on the summit of which they had built a Lamasery, (about 110 years ago). This the Gúrkhas had, more than once, attacked and plundered, and, at one time, had converted it into one of their guard posts. The ruin of the Lamasery remains to the present day. The name, "*Dorjeling*" was given by the Tibetans; it is compounded of three words; viz. རྡོ *rdo* a stone, རྗེ *rje* noble, and གླིང *gling* a place. The first two words compose a compound word, རྡོ་རྗེ *dor-rje* a precious stone, a jewel, also a meteorite stone; hence, an ecclesiastical sceptre, (emblematical of the thunderbolt, Sanscrit वज्र); so, རྡོ་རྗེ་གླིང *Dor-rje-gling*, pronounced Dorjeling, (corrupted, by Europeans, to Darjeeling), may be translated—the place of ecclesiastical sway.

beautiful and convenient spot, for a sanatarium, and strongly urged on Government the importance of securing it for that purpose. The then Governor-General Lord Bentinck, and his successor Lord Auckland, both appreciated the advantage of holding such a position in the hills, and both earnestly commended it to the attention of the Court of Directors. The latter, in the year 1830, forwarded directions that, on the first favourable opportunity, overtures should be made to the Sikim Ruler for the cession of the Hill of Dorjeling. In 1834, boundary disputes having again risen between Nepal and Sikim, Major Lloyd, as Governor-General's Agent, was deputed to settle affairs, and to treat for the surrender of the Hill tract of Dorjeling. The king consented to cede the land, on condition that the territory of Debgang, (with one or two other minor stipulations), should be granted to him in exchange. In reply, it was represented, that as this property had already been conferred on the Rajah of Julpai-gúri, it was impossible to accede to his desire. The answer returned was, simply, an unconditional present of the côveted land. The English version of the transfer deed, as rendered by the Government translators, being short, I here give it verbatim.

Translation of the Deed of Grant making over Dorjeling to the East India Company, dated 29th Magh, Sambat 1891, = A. D. February, 1835.

'The Governor-General having expressed his desire for the possession of the 'Hill of Dorjeling, on account of its cool climate, for the purpose of enabling the 'servants of his Government, suffering from sickness, to avail themselves of its ad-'vantages, I, the King of Dre-jong* (translated Sikimputti Rajah), out of friendship 'to the said Governor-General, hereby present Dorjeling to the East India Company, 'that is, all the land south of the Great Rung-nyit (translated Rungeet) River, east 'of the Ru-shi (translated Balasun), Kalyail and Little Rung-nyit (translated Run-'geet) Rivers, and west of the (translated) Rungus† and Mahanuddi Rivers.'

Major Lloyd was commissioned to construct roads, and to make all arrangements for establishing an European settlement. Under his administration all that was undertaken succeeded, and entire harmony existed with Sikim. In 1839, Colonel Lloyd left Dorjeling on active military employ, and Dr. Campbell who had previously served at Kathmandah, was temporarily appointed in his room, and afterwards permanently confirmed as Superintendent of Dorjeling. He was vested with extraordinary and independent judicial powers.

---

* འབྲས་ལྗོངས *hbras-ljongs*, pronounced, as above, Drejong (literally, the country of rice), the name given to the country by the Tibetans, called by Gúrkhas, and, hence, improperly, by Europeans—Sikim.

† Meaning the Rung-nyo; (called by Gúrkhas, and now *improperly*, as in the above note, by Europeans,—Teestah).

Having thus given an outline of the events which preceded and led to the occupation of the British in Sikim, we may take a glance at the people and country, of whom, and of which, the British Government took the charge. Towards showing in a slight degree the characteristics of the Lepchas, and the state in which we found them, I shall, here, make a short extract from a letter I wrote, twenty years ago, regarding them, to a gentleman high in Government administration.

"What or whersoever might have been their original source, they here appeared in the most simple, primitive state, living in the midst of the vast, wild, magnificent forests, old as the hills themselves, and, as I think, I mentioned to you, each family residing by itself, having no villages or communities, and but little intercourse with each other; thus they dwelt in pretty cottages, around which they cultivated their plot of ground, which afforded them rice,—their staple food;—grain of different sorts; cotton, from which they spun their cloth; seeds from which they expressed their oil, &c. From the forests they obtained fruits of numerous descriptions, edible and otherwise useful; thus all their wants were supplied. They knew no care, and but little sorrow, cheerful as the birds, and sturdy as the trees around them, they roamed through the forests inhaling health. They understood little about medicines and had not much use for them, sickness being almost unknown among them, but they possess some very efficacious roots, &c., with which I believe Europeans are still unacquainted. Their religion was particularly simple; they believed in one Good Spirit, and in innumerable evil spirits; to the former they conceived their worship was due, and to Him they offered their prayers and thanksgivings; the latter they considered prowled about, and haunted every spot; to them they attributed whatever sickness or misfortune befell, therefore deemed it requisite to propitiate them, which they did by offerings of rice, &c. The first fruits of the season were always offered to the Good Spirit. I may state that the purity of their belief was, at a period antecedent to our arrival, somewhat perverted by the introduction from Tibet of the Buddhist religion; it had and still has, however, but little hold on them."

Having no written, or authentic traditional records regarding their migration into this country, I have not yet been able to discover the exact period at which they first arrived. That they are in no way allied to any of the aboriginals of this country, is certain, nor can I find that they have any relationship with any of the immigrant races. They are called Môn by the Tibetans, which circumstance and a resemblance in physical conformation, might lead to the inference that consanguinity would be found to exist between them and the Môn race, the early settlers in Pegu,* but as far as I can judge from a comparison of their languages, the races are

* In the Asiatic Society's Journal, Major General Sir A. Phayre, K. C. S. I., C. B., writing on the

perfectly distinct. The Lepchas are naturally fair, latterly the absence of all forest shade, and intermarriage with the Yakthúmbha,* also, lately, with the Gúrkha races, have tended in a great measure, to alter the features and complexions of many families.

The earliest veritable information I can acquire of their history, commences from the time of their King Turvè (ᰊᰪᰲ ᰚᰬ ᰎ ᰍᰨ *Tur-vè pa-no*), who, apparently, reigned about 450 years ago, and about this period, they, probably, entered the country. Midst the extensive forests which covered the entire southern face of the Himalayahs, and which, in Sikim, from the firs and pines and scant verbage that skirts the eternal snows, to the dense luxuriant tropical vegetation of the vallies, were then totally uninhabited, the homeless Lepchas found what they sought, a place of refuge. They gave to the country the appellation of *ne lyáng* (ᰍᰬ ᰜᰠᰦᰵ), literally, a place of caves, hence, of retreat, of shelter, (so, Tib. གནས་པ a place, a residence གནས་པར *gnas-par,* to dwell, to abide); and caves, (some of which, in Sikim, are very extensive), may, for a space of time, have been their chief habitations. In this land, they settled down, cultivating the soil in peace and tranquillity. Whatever may have been their previous circumstances, adversities and troubles, they, here, found a haven of rest. After the death of King Turvè, three successive Lepchas,† sons of their Royal Fathers, ruled the land. In the meantime the people had prospered and increased. But this halcyon state was not permitted to progress, altogether, undisturbed.

On the demise of King Tur-ayek, the throne was usurped by a Tibetan,‡ from

History of Pegu, remarks, with reference to the connection of the Môn with other tribes, the fact, that, 'Csoma de Koros, in his Tibetan Dictionary, defines Mon as a general name for the hill people between Tibet and the plains of India.' The Tibetans, at Dorjeling, apply the term to the Lepchas alone, they do not call the Nepalese, or other tribes— མོན *Môn.*

* This race, generally known to Europeans as the Limbú, is a peculiar one. The people are Hindus in religion, but less bigoted than the Gúrkhas. Though some of the words in their language, are allied to Lepcha, the tongues are altogether dissimilar; and the people are darker and very inferior to the Lepchas. Formerly they possessed a written character of their own, which Dr. Campbell, in 1850, informed me, had long died out, and that he had, in vain, endeavoured to find traces of it. In 1853, while in the hills, I came across a man who possessed some books and could read and write; from him I acquired a knowledge of the caligraphy. At Dr. Campbell's request, I gave him a copy of the Alphabet. On my return from England in 1857, I found in an old number of the Journal of the Asiatic Society of Bengal, published during my absence, a description and lithograph of the Alphabet, but the latter rendered upside-down and otherwise incorrect.

† Their several names were, ᰊᰪᰲ ᰛᰦᰵ ᰎ ᰍᰨ *Tur-sáng pa-no,* ᰊᰪᰲ ᰣᰬᰵ ᰎ ᰍᰨ *Tur-ageng pa-no,* and ᰊᰪᰲ ᰣᰬᰭ ᰎ ᰍᰨ *Tur-agek pa-no.*

‡ His name and title were, ཕུན་ཚོགས་རྣམ་རྒྱལ *phún-tshogs rnam-rgyas, (Phún-tsho Nam-gye),* and those of his successors, (in what may be termed the Tibeto-Lepcha dynasty), were, རྟེན་སྲུང་རྣམ་རྒྱལ *rten-súng rnam-rgyas, (Ten-súng Nam-gye);* ཕྱག་རྡོར་རྣམ་རྒྱལ *phyag-rdor rnam-rgyas, (Chak-dor Nam-gye);* འགྱུར་མེད་རྣམ་རྒྱལ

which period a new era commences. He and his successors, however, married Lepchas, and the language and customs of the latter were retained. But other circumstances supervened to detract from the happy state of primitiveness in which the Lepchas lived. After the Tibetan usurpation of the throne, the Buddhists of Tibet began to enter Sikim, and to found lamaseries therein. In these, as usual, they stocked and reared young neophites, and thence they disseminated their doctrines. In essaying to proselytize the people, they were not at all scrupulous as to their mode of conversion. They collected and destroyed the manuscript books of the Lepchas; and translated into Lepcha parts of their own mythological works, under the name of Tashi-sung, (History of Tashi), thus giving the pure and unsullied name of Tashi,* (which single and invisible God, the Lepchas had hitherto worshipped with all the simplicity and purity of children), to a foul and fabulous incarnation, whose pretended life, they published, and this, (with the indoctrination of a host of other deities), they preached to the Lepchas as gospel. Jealousy and rancour, also, rose between the rulers and chiefs, which by no means added

---

hgyúr-met rnam-rgyas, (*Gyúr-met Nam-gye*); རྣམ་རྒྱས་ཕུན་ཚོགས *rnam-rgyas phún-tshogs*, (*Nam-gye Phún-tsho*); བརྟེན་འཛིན་རྣམ་རྒྱས *brten-hdsôn rnam-rgyas*, (*Ten-zôn Nam-gye*. It was in this king's reign that the lamasery at Dorjeling was built, he afterwards died at Lhasa); གཙུག་ཕུད་རྣམ་རྒྱས *gtsúg-phút rnam-gyas*, (*Tsúk-phút Nam-gye*); and the 8th and present ruler, སྲིད་སྐྱོང་སྐུ་གཞོགས *srid-skyong sku-gzhogs*, (*Sit-kyong Ku-zho*), His Majesty, the defender of the realm. Since writing the above I have heard of the death of this king. Lately he had been acting with considerable independence — the Lamas were, consequently, much dissatisfied with him.

* His title is ᰊᰡᰧ ᰊᰪᰭᰓᰨ ᰋᰧᰵ *Ta-shi Tuk-bo Thing*, compounded of ᰊ *ta*, a prefixed particle, here forming a substantive; ᰡᰧ *shi*, to see; this is also often, especially since the ingress of Tibetans pronounced *she*, from ᰡᰬ *she*, (Tib. ཤེས་པར *shes-par*), to know; synonymous with, to see; ᰡᰧᰜᰬ *shi re*, the sight, *scire* to know, to ken, (compare, Goth. *kann*, Tib. མཁྱེན Lep. ᰁᰥᰬᰰ *Khyen*, to know, also Lep. ᰀᰨ *ko*, to comprehend, to be cunning; (whence also, English *can*, Lep. ᰁᰪ *khu* to be able, ᰀᰨᰰ *kón* to cause]; Lith. *zi-noti*, Dutch *zee*, Tib. གཟིགས་པར *gzigs-par*, (*zi*-par), Lep. ᰛᰪ *zu*, to see, to perceive, to know by seeing, &c.); *tuk-bo*, the agentive of ᰊᰪᰭ *tuk*, to overspread, (compare, Heb. טח Arab. طاق a covering, a cupola &c.); and ᰋᰧᰵ *thing*, a lord, (radically implying, an exalted flow from the First Cause, (see also, lord, in Powers of Letters), relatively, being a reduced participial form of ᰋᰧ *thi*, to reach, to arrive at, whence co-relatively we have Sax. *thincg*, the *thing* emphatically, serving (ᰊᰬᰭ ᰇᰩᰰ *tek-hán*), progressing, from lowest to highest, the *thane*; the *thoht*, having its seat in ᰋᰤᰩᰭ *thyák*, the head, (hence *thyák*, also signifies, to know, ᰋᰤᰨ *thyo*, to hear, to know, to know by hearing), leading to the ᰋᰨᰭ *thok*, the highest point; the ᰋᰩᰲ *thár*, the goal, the תאר working on to the θάνατος, or to θεός. See *Th*, in Powers of Letters). Hence, *Ta-shi Tuk-bo Thing* signifies, the All-seeing, Omniscient and Omnipresent Lord.

to their tranquillity; these fomented, and excited their passions, till, in 1825, these latter burst forth with violence. The then ruler, Tsuk-phut Nam-gye, suspecting, with reason or otherwise, his chief minister, a Lepcha, by name Rá-thup, of conspiring with the Gúrkhas to dethrone him, made a sudden onslaught and slew several of his relatives. The Chief himself, with his adherents, succeeded in escaping to Ilám,—a district on the Eastern frontier of Nepal,—where their descendants still form a settlement.

All this, however, chiefly effected the *Bar-fóng-mo*,* and the few chiefs about the court; it made little impression on the mass of the people, these still followed their own habits and customs, still lived untrammelled in the vast forests, they yet had their priests—the bards; and the squabbles of the court, and the teachings of the Buddhists were of little import. The advent of the Europeans was the first real blow the Lepchas received; their downfall quickly followed. Dr. Campbell, on obtaining the government, used his influence to induce every foreign tribe, and people, to come and settle in the country to the great detriment of the Lepchas. The Gúrkhas, whom the British had such trouble in expelling from the territory, were particularly encouraged; they, the Múrmis,† and innumerable other tribes flocked into the land, they settled whither they willed, they burned down the forests, the country became filled with them. To avoid the odious association of the Gúrkhas, who were ever their enemies, and whose habits and customs, with their narrow-minded cold-blooded dispositions, degrading and baneful caste prejudices were totally at variance with the open warm-hearted spirits, and overflowing generous character of the Lepchas,‡ the latter fled from place to place, cultivation became neglected, want and misery ensued. Ground-rent, in specie, was also demanded; how was this to be paid by those, who, until Europeans arrived, had never seen money, never known what it was. Their happy and peaceful homes, (homes, which were most hospitably and disinterestedly thrown open to all comers), were lost to them for ever. Broken-hearted, many of the elders died. The younger resorted to the station of Dorjeling, there, as the state of affairs was, their destruction became a matter of certainty. They arrived artless innocent children, all they saw and heard was new

---

* The Lepchas observe two chief degrees of rank, (each of which has its own gradations), viz., the *bar-fóng-mo*; and the *á-den*, (the power of letters implying, 'the flowing from on High;' and 'the created, fashioned, formed'), the aristocracy, and commoners; the patricians, and plebeians.

† The Múrmi, a low tribe inhabiting Eastern Nepal. They have a dialect of their own, and profess a religion between Buddhism and Hinduism; they are held in small esteem, both by the Buddhists of Tibet and by the Hindus of Nepal; they bear a dreadful name of being murderers, they themselves have a saying, 'before we steal we kill.'

‡ One of their many amiable traits, and one which I never found wanting, even in children, was, that they never received anything without sharing it with a companion.

to them, ignorant of the Hindustani language, here introduced, totally inexperienced, unsuspecting, trusting, they at once fell a prey to the designing. Bereft of the few articles they had brought with them, starvation stared them in the face. To obtain food they were forced to perform work from which their spirit recoiled; they were reduced to become bearers of burdens, to take to working on the roads. They were in manners and customs and in true civilization immeasurably superior to any of the surrounding tribes, to the Gúrkhas, or to the natives of the plains. The two latter were set over them as task-masters. The Lepchas, the free sons of the forests, the hearty yeoman of the land, the lords of the soil, became the servants of servants, the very slaves of slaves. The lot of those who fell into household employment was no better. Few good natives of the plains at this time ever ventured to Dorjeling; it was notorious as a place of refuge for the out-pouring of jails, as a resort of all the most profligate and abandoned. These became the masters and teachers of the Lepchas. With such tuition, is it surprising that the latter should have become learned in all duplicity and every vice? The women also, naturally exceedingly gentle and modest, became the victims of the licentious:—the fall of the Lepchas was complete.

Other causes were, also, tending to the destruction of the Lepcha nationality. The Lepcha language which had, hitherto, been the language of the whole country of Sikim, which all Tibetans, Bútias,* or others who entered the country acquired and

---

* All the Tibetan settlers, south of the Himalayahs from Ladak eastward, are denominated by Europeans, Bútias, (derived from the Tibetan word བོད་ *Bôd,* the true name of Tibet). They are called by the Tibetans, ལྷོ་པ་ *Lho-pa,* southerners or southmen. There is a large settlement of them in the hills east of Sikim, the country is called by Europeans, Bútan. It is named by Lepchas ᰎᰥᰫ *Prú,* (derived from འབྲུག་པ *hbrug-pa* a schismatic sect of the Búddhists, to which the Bútias belong), and the settlers are designated ᰣᰦᰛᰦᰳ *á-rát.* They are physically large and powerfully built, much more so than their progenitors the Tibetans, but in mental qualities they have proportionately degenerated; neither the people nor the Government have improved by time.

The first connection the Indian Government had with Bútan, was in 1772, when Kúch Behar being overrun and devastated by the Bútias, the Nazah Deo appealed to the British for protection. Troops consisting only of two companies of Sipahis and two pieces of cannon, under command of a Captain Jones, was despatched. This small force without any difficulty took the chief town of Kúch Behar then occupied by the Bútias, reduced the forts of Daling, &c., and clearing all before them, drove the Bútias into their fastnesses. (This offers a grave contrast with the management of later days, as exemplified when troops were sent to enter Sikim in the end of 1848, and in the expensive Bútan campaign of 1865-66). The Bútias applied to Tibet for assistance; the, then, Tashi Lama forwarded a solicitation for peace, expressed in language so modest and superior, so free from the obsequiousness or bombast peculiar to Oriental despatches, as immediately to attract the attention of Warren Hastings; a treaty very favourable to Bútan was drawn up and ratified by the Governor-General in Council on the 25th April, 1774. By the first clause, all the lands, that belonged to the Bútias before their aggressions on Kúch Behar, were restored to them. On the following month Mr. George Bogle was despatched on a friendly mission to the Tashi Lama, (who was at that time, also, Regent of Tibet). He without difficulty reached Tashi lhún-po, (བཀྲས་ཤིས་ལྷུན་པོ་ *b-kras-shis lhún-po,* corrupted by Europeans to Tashoo Loomboo),

spoke, in which under the rule of Colonel Lloyd, business was carried on, and justice in the English Courts administered, in the character of which, decrees and documents were written and recorded ;—this language was completely set aside, and Hindustani was made the chief language in Dorjeling. The Tibetans and the Bútias of Bútan were patronized, to them were given the appointments in the administration of the country, and they were made the advisers and counsellors of the State ; their influx into Sikim increased. This was playing into the hands of the crafty priests, who already held the king in their thraldom ; their power and authority augmented. Oppressed and crushed on all sides, the Lepcha race and language came to be considered unfashionable. Many of the Lepchas intermarried with Bútias, and, repudiating their own race, denominated themselves Bútias.* The Tibetan language became the medium of communication between the Sikim and Dorjeling Governments. Dr. Campbell was, and his successors in the administration of Dorjeling, also, have all been, quite unacquainted with the Tibetan or Lepcha languages. Who then were the secretaries who wrote, and the interpreters who translated the correspondence ? In Sikim communications were written by the authority of the Tibetan conclave that surrounded the king, and in Dorjeling they were translated and answers sent by the

---

the cumulation of glory. He met with the most cordial reception from the Lama, and resided with him for nearly a year, experiencing unremitting attention and friendliness. Before Mr. Bogle's return, the Tashi Lama was exerting his influence for opening an unrestricted commerce between India and Tibet, He afterwards, and unfortunately before this important project had been secured, died of small-pox at Piking, where he had gone at the earnest request of the Emperor Kyen Lung to assist in the celebration on the occasion of his, (the Emperor's,) birth-day. As being the most enlightened ruler that probably Bútan or Tibet ever possessed, his title of དབང་སྐུ་ཞོགས *dbang skú-zhogs*, the Lord of Power, deserves to be recorded. Since his death the country has by no means improved. Other missions have proceeded to Bútan ; Capt. Turner's in 1783, Capt. Pemberton's in 1838, and the Hon'ble Ashley Eden's in 1863-64,—none receiving the friendly reception accorded to Mr. Bogle, but each encountering increased difficulties. Their reports have been published and may be referred to by those interested in the subject. The occurrences of the Bútan campaign of 1865-66, &c., must be known to those who review the events of the passing day. But all these political acquisitions and military advances have in no ways tended to improve Bútan. In 1786, the Músalman Púringír Ghosain, who was the bearer of the letter from the Tashi Lama to Warren Hastings, and who afterwards accompanied Capt. Turner in his mission, deposed, that many merchants from Bengal had succeeded in reaching Tashi Lhúnpo, and that there was no scarcity of English goods there in the market. Though many Bútias are, individually, very amiable, still he would be a rash trader who would now (in 1874) venture, unprotected, to enter Bútan.

The language of Bútan is a corrupt Tibetan ; at least according to the pronunciation of the modern Tibetan tongue. It has no separate written character, so in reading the Bútias pronounce the same word quite differently than when talking ; thus, བྱ *bya*, a bird, would in speaking be pronounced, *pya*, but when reading they give it the Tibetan pronunciation of *cha*.

* These are the people whom Europeans designate as the naturalized Bútias of Sikim.

official Tibetans and Bútias, mere accomplices and creatures of the Sikim usurpers; or what was worse, by Lepcha apostates, traitors to their king and country, betrayers of their people, very Judases in spirit, worthy disciples of their Bútia and Hindustani teachers.* Such was the sole medium of communication with Sikim. Into the hands of these people were submitted for translation all the views, edicts and wishes of the British Government. Even had these interpreters been willing, they were quite incapable of performing the duties required. Possessed of the slightest smattering of Hindustani, from, and into which language they were expected to translate all communications, it was impossible they could translate correctly. Nor if capable, would they have presumed to have forwarded to the Sikim authorities a literal version of any documents offensive to them, directly authoritative, or in which censure was conveyed. At all events the Tibetan documents have been sealed books to the representatives of the British Government at Dorjeling. Under such a system how could it be hoped that administration could be satisfactorily conducted.

In 1849, Dr. Campbell, proceeding into Sikim, (to join Dr. Hooker, who was then making a tour in that country), was seized by the Bútias and severely maltreated, nearly losing his life. He attributed this assault to revenge for his having refused to return to the owners, the slaves† who had fled from Sikim to the British territory of Dorjeling. Slaves of whom?—Of the Bútias who attacked him, of those whose settlement and influence in the country had been promoted

---

* This may appear an unnecessary effusion of epithets, but, if sentiments are to be expressed by words, the language will not be considered too strong when it is known, that, on expostulating with one of these persons, (a Lepcha interpreter of the Court, the only interpreter of Lepcha, a man who can neither read nor write, selected for this important and responsible employment, by the Superintendent of Dorjeling), for not endeavouring to support and preserve his own language and people, I was told by him, that his language and people might go to perdition as long as he gained money. It may be truly said, that the man was ignorant, and his words beneath notice; but he should not therefore have been placed in the position he was, and in which he is still retained.

† Two of Dr. C.'s (and I believe the sole) remarks condemnatory of the Lepchas were, that they had slaves, and that they did not speak the truth. Regarding the first, the Lepchas, certainly possessed people of their own race employed as 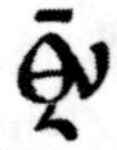 *vyet*, slaves or servants, and so have had all people, in all ages. Degree exists amongst all animate beings, inanimate matter finds its level. Our great dramatic poet makes Agamemnon say, 'Take but degree away, remove that string, and hark what discord follows:' we are, also, told in Scripture, that degree finds its order in Heaven. It is not the use, but the abuse of slaves, as exemplified in their treatment by the Romans and in America, &c., that has brought odium on the name. The Lepchas put themselves into voluntary bondage for a period, (as did the Patriarchs,) serving for their wives. The friendless, the orphans, the needy and helpless found shelter, food, and comfort in the houses of the more prosperous; there were no poor in the land. The so-called slaves of the Lepchas were far more

by the encouragement given, and by the policy pursued by Dr. Campbell himself? To avenge the outrage committed, troops were sent to Dorjeling, but they never entered Sikim. Government contented itself by confiscating the whole of the Sikim territories south of the Rumám and west of the Rungnyit rivers, and by stopping the annual allowance of Rs. 6,000, which was granted to the king, (3,000, in 1841, and an additional 3,000, in 1846), as a slight compensation for his cession of the territory in 1835.

For years after this, the entrance of travellers into Sikim was closed by the Sikim Government. In 1860, Dr. Campbell, having reported to Government, a case of kidnapping, and violence, committed by the Bútias, recommended part of the territories north of the river Rumám to be taken possession of, until such time as the offenders should be given up by the Sikim Government. With the object of carrying this into effect, Dr. C. with a detachment of Sebundy Sappers and Miners, and a 6℔. gun, crossed the Rumám. The Bútias, however, mustered a force and overpowering the Sappers, who ran short of ammunition, obliged them to retreat. They followed up their success, burning some police stations in British territory, and even threatened Dorjeling. A force (consisting of a detachment of Royal Artillery with 3 guns; wings of H. M. 6th foot; 73rd N. I.; and 3rd Sikh Infantry; also detachments of the 1st, Bat. Bengal Police, and of the Sebundy Sappers and Miners),

free than the dependents or the mercenary hirelings of civilized countries; they were treated in every respect as one of the family, they and their masters worked, eat, and in all things shared alike, I never knew or heard of any of these servitors who ever wished to leave their homes. The fate of the slaves of the more imperious Bútias (though I never witnessed any maltreatment), may perhaps have been different. But the novelty and vanities of Dorjeling were the true causes of their flight thither. What protection, however, did such Lepchas, who were supposed to seek refuge in Dorjeling, receive. Being initiated into the use of money, taught to consider it the one thing needful, and finding it the only means of obtaining food, both masters and dependents became slaves to one of the most exacting and oppressive of tyrants. Upon them were heaped all the artificial wants, all the load of necessities and miseries emanating from a pseudo state of civilization. They were taken from their calm flow of existence and plunged into a troubled sea of passions, in which, before the eyes of heedless spectators, they have been allowed to sink and perish.

As to Dr. Campbell's second cause of censure, I can affirm I ever found the Lepchas most honest and truthful. I do not speak for the veracity of those who were taught, and whose characters were moulded, in Dorjeling, but of the Lepchas in their simple state. I would refer and recommend to the readers of this, Hooker's most interesting journal in Sikim. In it the learned Doctor enters with quite enthusiasm, into the gentle honest character of the Lepchas. Speaking of them, he says, "In disposition they are amiable and obliging, frank, humorous and polite, without the servility of the Hindóos, and their address is free and unconstrained. Their intercourse with one another and with Europeans is scrupulously honest." ******* "A more interesting and attractive companion than the Lepcha I never lived with." ******* "Ever foremost in the forest or in the bleak mountain, and ever ready to help to carry, to encamp, to collect, or to cook, they cheer on the traveller by their unostentatious zeal, and are spurs to his progress." &c. General Lloyd and all who formerly knew the Lepchas ever spoke of them with the highest esteem. The Hon'ble Ashley Eden, who as Envoy accompanied the force, in 1861, to Tamlúng, in an able report does justice to the probity and integrity of the Lepcha character.

was speedily assembled. This force entered Sikim, on the 2nd February, 1861, and without opposition, (except a slight skirmish on crossing the Rung-nyit, in which, on our side, only one man was killed and two men wounded,) arrived, in March, at *Taṃ-lóng*, the capital of Sikim. All that was demanded was acceded to, a treaty, containing 23 articles, being signed by the king. The causers of all this disturbance, (the kidnappers,) however were never surrendered ; they had, or were said to have escaped into Prú (Bútan). The British Government has again conferred on the Sikim Ruler an annual and larger allowance, to be enjoyed as long as order is maintained in his dominions. Since then the country has become more tranquil and, as far as the snows (but no farther), is again thrown open to visitors. Sikim, however, is fast deteriorating. The influx of the Butians has increased, and the power of the Budhists has become firmly established ; the Gúrkhas have also commenced to settle in it, and the grandest and most glorious scenery in the world is becoming completely destroyed.* With the destruction of the forests in Sikim, the charm of the country will pass away, the climate will change,† and unless speedy

---

* Utterly reckless, for the sake of a small space of ground for cultivation, they set fire to, and burn down all the surrounding forests.

† I cannot, here, refrain from quoting a passage from Huc and Gabet's Travels in Tartary, &c., as the description so exactly coincides with what Dorjeling was, and with what it is becoming ; though it is to be hoped it will never be reduced to the exceeding calamitous state represented in the sketch. Referring to a district in the kingdom of Onniot, Huc says,—

" Towards the middle of the 17th century, the Chinese began to penetrate into the district. At that " period it was still one of rude grandeur ; the mountains were covered with fine forests, and the Mongol " tents whitened the valleys, amid rich pasturages. For a very moderate sum the Chinese obtained per- " mission to cultivate the desert, and as cultivation advanced the Mongols were obliged to retreat, conducting " their flocks and herds elsewhere.

" From that time forth the aspect of the country became entirely changed. All the trees were grubbed " up, the forests disappeared from the hills, the prairies were cleared by means of fire, and the new cultivators " set busily to work in exhausting the fecundity of the soil. Almost the entire region is now in the hands " of the Chinese, and it is probably to their system of devastation that we must attribute the extreme irregu- " larity of the seasons which now desolate this unhappy land. Droughts are of almost annual occurrence ; " the spring winds setting in dry up the soil, * * * * * *. Next after these hurricanes comes the " rain ; but so comes, that instead of being an object of desire, it is an object of dread, for it pours down " in furious raging torrents. * * * * The torrent rushes on and in a few hours the earth reappears ; " but the crops are gone, and worse even than that, the arable soil also has gone with them. * * * * * " The droughts and the inundations together sometimes occasion famines which well-nigh exterminate the " inhabitants. That of 1832 in the twelfth year of the reign of *Tao-Kouóng*, is the most terrible of these " on record." After relating the apprehensions and forebodings of the people ; he continues,—" The fearful " prognostic that had been so often repeated became accomplished. Thousands died upon the hills, * * * " whole villages were depopulated * * *. It was in this dismal region that we awaited, &c."

No one, who knew Dorjeling as it was, and who can comtemplate it as it is, on reading the above narration, would fail to be most painfully impressed with the similarity in the state of the two countries.

measures be taken to prevent it, the Lepchas will pine, and in time cease to exist. Much more might be said, but enough has been represented to account for the deplorable fall of the Lepchas.

Of the language I cannot speak too highly. The simple and primitive state in

---

Not content with the numerous tribes that had flocked into the land and ruined the Lepchas, Government, at the instance of Dr. C. issued an enactment whereby, the forest lands of Dorjeling were to be conferred on all who might apply for them. The terms were most inviting,—five years free, and afterwards the lands to be retained on nominal rental;—adventurers of all sorts, rich and poor cropped up, who with avidity accepted the terms, and seized on the lands. Tea-planting was introduced, the demand for land gradually increasing, till tea-planting became a passion, a mania, which infected all classes. Wealthy companies were formed, lands exchanged hands at exorbitant prices, the money not flowing into the Government coffers, but enriching the speculators, who retired with large fortunes. The few forests, spared by the Gúrkhas, &c., speedily disappeared. The effect on the Lepchas was most disastrous. The residents and planters are also beginning to feel the results. In Dorjeling wood, for fuel and domestic purposes, can, now, hardly be obtained, whence are planters to procure it to supply the large consumption necessary to feed their furnaces, &c.? The heavy tropical rains wash from the slopes of the hills the arable soil, unless surrounding woods are left standing, where is fresh mould to come from? The Dorjeling hills are already becoming comparatively unproductive. Formerly Dorjeling was noted for the excellency of it's vegetable productions, now those produced are very inferior. The forests being cleared, the land absorbs the hot rays of the sun, rendering the soil arid. Snow, which used to be abundant at Dorjeling, now scarcely ever falls. The salubrity of the climate, as a matter of course, has become much impaired. Besides the ailments thereby induced, the country has been, also, subjected to the introduction of numerous maladies consequent on an artificial and gregarious mode of existence. Even the common Asiatic disease of cholera, was formerly unknown to the Lepchas. In 1872 the workmen on the gardens of the planters were nearly decimated by it. The cattle disease, with which the Lepchas were also unacquainted, has likewise several times made its appearance, brought up by the bullocks from the plains, almost exterminating the fine cattle of the hills.

I cannot close this subject without saying a word, the result of my experience, in favour of trees,—the adornment of the earth, which occupies the rank, in the vegetable world, that man inherits in the animal kingdom,—which it is now the custom of Dendrophobists everywhere to fell. In damp and confined places, where decomposition of vegetable matter, water, and earth abounds, giving rise to carbonic acid, and other deleterious gases, more than the living vegetation can absorb, malaria will be generated. Sufficient living vegetation, especially high trees, will inhale these gases, exhaling, in their room, particularly in the day, life-giving oxygen. In the hills, where the forests are so thick as to be impervious to the penetrating rays of a tropical sun, malarious fevers are unknown. Even Dr. Campbell,—no friend of trees or forests,—in a published account of a journey in the hills, says, (I speak from memory, not having seen the article since it was first published, upwards of 20 years ago,) that he was encamped in the forests where the effluvia arising from decayed and rank vegetation were so excessive as to be suffocating, still, though very subject to fever, he never experienced the slightest attack.

Sikim, after the Nepalese had been driven out, ought to have been restored to it's original and rightful owners, the Lepchas. Their sway, and natural innocence and purity ought to have been beneficently upheld. The magnificent forests of Magnolias, Rhododendrons, and rare and invaluable trees ought to have been

which the Lepchas lived is admirably shown by it. It has no primary words (beyond the words for gold and silver) to express money, merchants or merchandise, fairs or markets. Their peaceful and gentle character is evinced by their numerous terms of tenderness and compassion, and by the fact that not one word of abuse exists in their language. Nevertheless the language itself is most copious, abounding in synonyms and possessing words to express every slightest change, every varying shade of meaning, it admits of a flow and power of speech which is wonderful, and which renders it capable of giving expression to the highest degree of eloquence. The language also attests the astonishing knowledge possessed by the Lepchas. I shall here again make an extract from the letter before quoted:—"Of all the almost inconceivable diversity of trees with which the hills are covered; of all the almost incalculable variety of plants and flowers with which the forests are filled; the Lepchas can tell you the names of all, they can distinguish at a glance the difference in the species of each genus of plants, which would require the skill of a practised botanist to perceive; and this information and nomenclature extends to beasts, to birds, to insects, and to everything around them, animate and inanimate; without instruction, they seem to acquire their knowledge by intuition alone. The trees and the flowers, and the birds, and the insects have heretofore been their friends and companions. But now, this simple knowledge, this beautiful language, this once happy people are fast dying out. The Lepchas have left their woods and innocence and have fallen into sin and misery, and is there no one that will help them, no one that will save?"

It is impossible that a people, with a language so comprehensive; with manners, though primitive, so superior, as to entitle them to rank high among civilized nations, could be engendered amidst the wilds and fastnesses of the Himalayahs. They retain, in so marked a degree, all the simple ways and habits of the patriarchs of old, as to lead to the conclusion, that they must have remained isolated ever since

---

most carefully guarded. For they,—with mountains, compared with whose high altitude the Alps shrink into insignificance, on whose lofty summits, towering above in everlasting snow, no human foot may ever tread, their dazzling whiteness and unapproachable exaltation, sublimely representing the purity and power of the Omnipotent,—all formed a scene unrivalled in grandeur; a scene, which a traveller, who had visited all parts of the world, on arriving at Dorjeling and viewing, in rapture exclaimed, in the words of Simeon of old,—'Now, let me die in peace, for I have seen the Glory of the Lord.' Dorjeling, in truth, was a very garden of Eden, a spot which God had blessed with transcendent loveliness, and as such ought to have been most religiously preserved from the desecrating hand of man. It was a special spot, where the care-worn, and those weary with the hollowness and vanities of the world might have turned to, and returned refreshed and invigorated, ennobled, for the true duties of life; a spot, on beholding which, the haughty and discontented alike, would have comprehended their own littleness and unworthiness, and would have bowed down in homage to, and adoration of, the Almighty Creator.

such customs were in vogue.* The type of their features indicates, that before settling in the Himalayahs, they had probably, resided in Mongolia or Manchuria, and in, or near one of these countries. the body of the people might still be found.† The language is a monosyllabic one, (though not altogether an isolating one, as it possess in a degree—as all languages however primitive do—an agglutinative structure), and is unquestionably far anterior to the Hebrew or Sanskrit. It is preeminently an *Ursprache*, being probably, and I think, I may, without fear of misrepresentation, state it to be, the oldest language extant. It is a most comprehensive and beautiful one; and regarded alone, as a prolific source of the derivations and etyma of words, it is invaluable to the philological world. It however recommends itself to us on higher grounds; it possesses and plainly evinces the principle and motive on which all language is constructed.‡ But, like everything really good in this world, it has been despised and rejected. To allow the Lepcha race, and language to die out would indeed be most barbarous, and inexpressibly sad.

---

* It may be noted, that the Lepchas, have legends,—in common with divers other primitive races, (which merit notice, as testifying to the truth of Sacred History),—regarding the flood and the Tower of Babel. The legends were, without doubt, brought with them from beyond the snows, but they have connected the incidents with their present place of residence.—There is a hill, visible from Dorjeling, (*tun-róng*), which, as the tale hath it, when all the country was under water, arose and supported a ship containing a few persons, all other people being drowned. The hill rose up like a horn, (hence its name, *á-róng*, a horn), and afterwards subsided to its present form. It is known to Europeans as the Camel's back.—On the top of the lofty *sung-li hlo*, it is said, a foolish class of Lepchas—(the *na-óng*), now extinct,—endeavoured to raise a building high enough to reach the heavens. Rock and blocks of stones, as the ruins, are shown on the place.

† The primitive Lepcha, probably, more comprehensive than we even at present find it, was in all likelihood, at an early period, the one, sole spoken language; and though both the people and language have long since been converted into different races and tongues; yet as we have found in the Sikim territory, one part of the race still intact, it is reasonable to suppose we may elsewhere discover another portion. The Altaic and Tungusian ranges, or even some of the yet unexplored districts of the Himalayahs offer a not unhopeful field of inquiry. There is in the Himalayahs, near Ladák, a tribe denominated Lapchas. Some years ago, when travelling through the latter country, I passed near the district in which they are settled. I had not time, however, to change my course, and I have not yet been able to obtain any information regarding the people or their language, to enable me to make a comparison betweén them and the Lepchas of Dorjeling.

‡ In the structure of the Lepcha language, I have discovered the system on which, I consider, all language is based. By an exegesis which I have, in part, prepared, (combined with a diagram showing the rudimental powers of letters), the roots and true significations of all words in all languages, are, at once, rendered apparent. Reference to this subject has several times been made in these pages, under the title of 'Powers of Letters.' I have not been able to complete the system, (as I wished) to accompany this Grammar, but (as I remark with regard to the Dictionary), should circumstances permit, it shall follow.

By the favour of the British Government in India, the writer has been enabled to present to the public a short Grammar of this language. (Should his health and circumstances permit, a Dictionary will follow.) The Grammar itself is simply written to assist the learner; it does not challenge the strictures of the critic; its mission is alone, to be useful, and should it conduce to the employment of a language and the amelioration of a people, both of which have been too long neglected, its object will be fully gained.

Calcutta, 1875.

INDEX.

E R R A T A.

Page x, line 9, from top, *for* verbage *read* herbage.

" xvi, " 2, from bottom, *for* Tamlúng, *read* Tamlóng.

" 6, " 14, from top, *for* 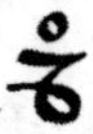 *read* 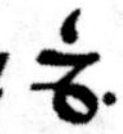.

" 8, " 14, " *for*  *read* 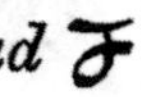; *for* 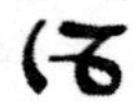 *read* 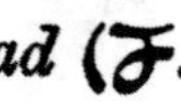.

" 8, " 7, from bottom, *for* 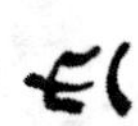 *read* .

" 9, " 2, from top, *for*  *read* .

" " " 14, " *for*  *read* 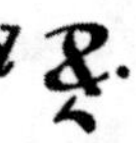.

" " " 16, " *for*  *read* 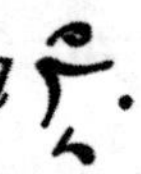.

" " " 3, from bottom, *for* fowl, *read* cow.

" " " 2, " *for* 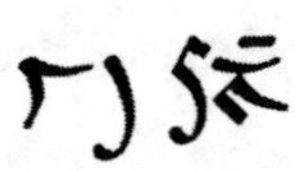 *read* 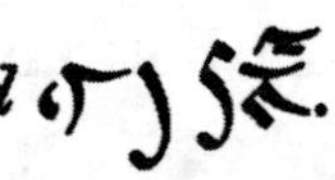.

" 11, " 3, from top, *for b dra b dra, read h dra h dra.*

" " " 11, " *for* 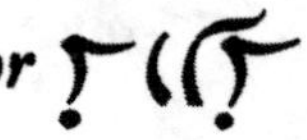 *read* 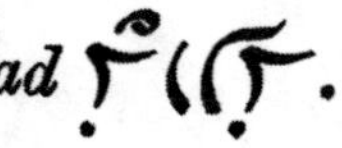.

" 16, " 14, " *for* krah *read* krak.

" 23, " 9, " *for*  *read* 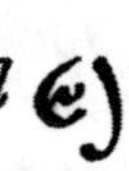; *for shú read shu.*

" 24, " 2, from bottom, *for* 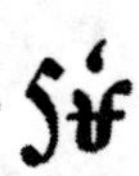 *read* 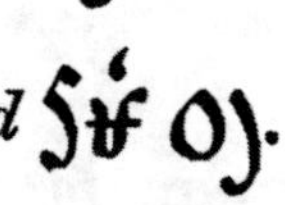.

" 29, " 12, from top, *for*  *read* 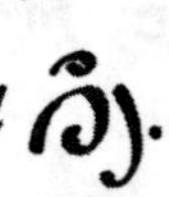.

" 29, " 2, from bottom, *for* 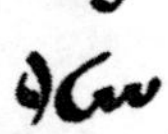 *read* 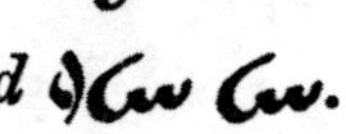.

" 35, " 18, from top, *for* 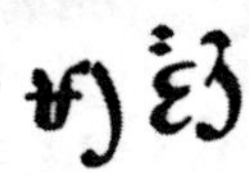 *read* 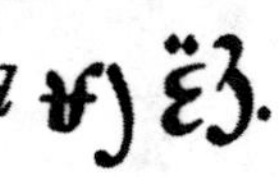.

Page 38, line 13, from top, [illegible] is upside down.

,, 41, ,, 1, ,, *for le.* Let *read le*, let.

,, ,, ,, 2, from bottom, *for* [illegible] *read* [illegible].

,, 50, ,, 6, from top, *for* [illegible] *nyet read* [illegible] *nyat.*

,, 50, ,, 7, ,, *for* [illegible] *nyet read* [illegible] *nyat*; (twice

,, 52, ,, 3, from bottom, *for* [illegible] *read* [illegible].

,, 57, ,, 8, from top, *for* [illegible] *read* [illegible].

,, 63, ,, 8, from bottom, *for* [illegible] *read* [illegible].

,, 64, ,, 4, ,, *for* [illegible] *read* [illegible].

,, 74, ,, 8, from top, *for* [illegible] *read* [illegible].

,, 75, ,, 9, from bottom, *for* [illegible] *read* [illegible].

,, 76, ,, 3, from top, *for* [illegible] *read* [illegible].

,, 78, ,, 4, ,, *for* [illegible] *read* [illegible]; *for* [illegible] *read* [illegible].

,, 78, ,, 3, from bottom, *for* tense *read* sense.

,, 81, ,, 5, from top, *erase* ~ *over* [illegible].

,, 84, ,, 6, ,, *erase* ~ *over bun.*

,, 84, ,, 5, from bottom, *for m t, read mát.*

,, 95, ,, 14, from top, *for* [illegible] *read* [illegible]; *for li mât, read lin mát.*

,, 99, ,, 5, ,, *for mán read man*; (twice).

,, 100, ,, 3, from bottom, *for* [illegible] *read* [illegible].

,, 106, ,, 7, from top, *for* [illegible] *chen read* [illegible] *chan, for* [illegible] *read* [illegible].

,, 106, ,, 11, ,, *for* [illegible] *chhok read* [illegible], *chho.*

,, 106, ,, 5, from bottom, *for* ni *read* in.

Page 109, line 14, from top, *for* [illegible] *read* [illegible].

„ 111, „ 14, „ *for* Noun. *read* Noun, &c.

„ 114, „ 6, „ *for* [illegible] *read* ([illegible].

„ 120, „ 8, from bottom, *for* [illegible] *read* [illegible].

„ 128, „ 4, „ *for* [illegible] *hu ká sa-thi zak*, *read* [illegible] [[illegible]] *hu ká thám mát* (*sa-thi zak*).

„ 129, „ 7, „ *for* sueceeded *read* succeeded.

„ 133, „ 2, from top, *for* [illegible] *read* [illegible].

„ 140, „ 13, „ *for* a week, *read* a week,).

*** There are other minor typographical errors, which I have not considered it necessary to insert in the errata; as, page 7, lines 7, 8, 22, a should be affixed to Ch, Chh, and Tsh; page 119, last line, a comma should be after Sakon. While the pages were passing through the Press, many errors occurred, a number of which were, through unavoidable circumstances, overlooked.

A

GRAMMAR

OF THE

RONG (LEPCHA) LANGUAGE.

PART I.

THE ALPHABET, *KAKHÓ RE.*

The Róng (Lepcha) Alphabet may be divided into two parts, *viz.*, Letters and Diacritical Marks, which latter include vowel, final, and other affixed signs.

These may be comprised, as follows:

Consonants,	35
Vowels,	8
Finals,	9
Kya and Kra, (affixed *y* and *r*)	2
Ṛ̃an (Circumflex sign),	1
Total,	55

The Consonants *ámo*, literally mother, chief, or large (letters), with their equivalents in Roman characters, are thus written.

1*st.*—THE CONSONANTS.

[illegible] *ámo re*, 35.

*K	Kh	G		Ng
ᰀ	ᰂ	ᰃ		ᰅ
Ch	Chh	J		Ny
ᰆ	ᰇ	ᰈ		ᰉ
T	Th	D		N
ᰊ	ᰋ	ᰌ		ᰍ
P	Ph	F	B	M
ᰎ	ᰐ	ᰑ	ᰓ	ᰕ
Ts	Tsh	Z		Y
ᰗ	ᰘ	ᰙ		ᰚ
R	L	H		V
ᰛ	ᰜ	ᰝ		ᰟ

S	Sh	W
ᰠ	ᰡ	ᰢ

Kl	Gl	Pl	Fl
ᰁ	ᰄ	ᰏ	ᰒ

Bl	Ml	Hl
ᰔ	ᰖ	ᰞ

* All these consonants have the sound of the inherent short *a* affixed to them.

DIACRITICAL MARKS,

called in Lepcha ᰋᰦᰮᰓᰤᰧᰰ *thámbyn*, (implying the vowel and final *signs, &c.).*

ᰣᰦᰀᰪᰱ ᰠ ᰋᰦᰮᰓᰤᰧᰰ ᰀᰀᰤᰭ ᰃᰪᰮ *ákup sa thámbyín kakyak gum*,

the Vowel Signs are seven in number, *viz.* :—

ᰦ ᰧ ᰨ ᰩ ᰪ ᰫ ᰬ

These are united to ᰣ *a*, the basis of all the vowels, as follows :

2*nd.*—THE EIGHT VOWELS.

* ᰣᰦᰀᰪᰱ ᰀᰀᰪ (᱈) ᰛᰬ *ákup kaku* (8) *re.*

A

ᰣ†

Á	*I*	*O*	*Ó*	*U*	*Ú*	*E*
ᰣᰦ	ᰣᰧ	ᰣᰨ	ᰣᰩ	ᰣᰪ	ᰣᰫ	ᰣᰬ

The vowel signs are similarly affixed to all the consonants.

3*rd.*—THE NINE FINALS.

ᰊᰬᰯᰓᰨ ᰠ ᰋᰦᰮᰓᰤᰧᰰ ᰀᰀᰤᰩᰳ (᱉) ᰛᰬ *Telbo sa thámbyn kakyót* **(9)** *re,*

the Final Signs are nine in number, and are thus formed,—

ᰭ ᰮ ᰯ ᰰ ᰱ ᰲ ᰳ ᰴ ᰵ

---

* This name ᰣᰦᰀᰪᰱ *ákup*, lit. child or small (letters), was formerly applied by the Lepchas exclusively to the Finals.

† This short a is inherent after all the consonants. The sound is effected by a simple (unaspirated) ejaculation of the breath.

Uniting these with ᰣ *a*, the basis of all the vowels, they, with their several names and pronunciations, stand thus—

Finals.	*Names.*	*Powers.*
ᰣᰭ ak	ᰜ ᰀᰦᰳ la kát	k
ᰣᰮ am	ᰜ ᰉᰳ la nyat	m
ᰣᰯ al	ᰜ ᰠᰦᰮ la sám	l
ᰣᰰ an	ᰍᰪᰰ nun	n
ᰣᰱ ab *or* ap	ᰓ ᰀᰪᰱ ba kup	b *or* p*
ᰣᰲ ar	ᰌᰲ dar	r
ᰣᰳ at	ᰀᰳ kat	t
ᰣᰵ ang	ᰀᰵ kang	ng
ᰣᰴ ang	ᰉᰧᰰᰌᰨ nyindó	ang

4*th.*—OF THE SIGNS (ᰋᰦᰮᰓᰤᰧᰰ *thámbyin*), ᰤ ᰀᰤ *KYA* and ᰥ ᰀᰥ *KRA.*

Like the Tibetan (ཡ་བཏགས *ya-btags* and ར་བཏགས *ra-btags*), the Lepcha language possesses an affixed *y* and *r*, thus—

ᰤ ᰀᰤ Kya

is affixed to the following twenty-three letters:

ᰀᰤ Kya ᰂᰤ Khya ᰃᰤ Gya ᰊᰤ Tya ᰋᰤ Thya
ᰌᰤ Dya ᰎᰤ Pya ᰐᰤ Phya ᰑᰤ Fya ᰓᰤ Bya
ᰕᰤ Mya ᰛᰤ Rya ᰜᰤ Lya ᰝᰤ Hya ᰟᰤ Vya
ᰁᰤ Klya ᰄᰤ Glya ᰏᰤ Plya ᰒᰤ Flya ᰔᰤ Blya
ᰖᰤ Mlya ᰞᰤ Hlya ᰣᰤ Aya

---

* Generally assumes the latter sound.

ြ Kra

Is affixed to eight letters thus—

ကြ Kra	ဂြ Gra	ငြ Ngra	ပြ Pra
ဖြ Fra	ဗြ Bra	မြ Mra	ဟြ Hra

And both are thus conjoined:

ကျြ Krya	ဂျြ Grya	ငျြ Ngrya	ပျြ Prya
ဖျြ Frya	ဗျြ Brya	မျြ Mrya	ဟျြ Hrya

With these signs, single or conjoined, the vowel and final signs are united.

5*th.*—OF THE SIGN (သာံ ပြင် *thambyin*).

~ ရံ *ṚÃN.*

There is a sort of circumflex sign, inscribed thus ~ called ရံ *Ṛãn*, (pronounced hard as if written dran*). This sign is supposed to be confined to the sole use of the two vowels အ *a* and ဣ *i*, but I have seen it written in books (though this is far from being any criterion of correctness) over the အာ *á*, and when necessary, it ought to be so applied; it would be useful in distinguishing the correct pronunciation, as for instance, in the words သာံ *sám*, three, and သာံ *sám*, to be sullen, (which latter might be written သာံ *sãm*). It is evidently the vowel sign ာ inverted over the vowel. Over ဣ it gives a prolonged sound as may be perceived in the difference between the words အာရိက် *árik*, a creeper (plant), and ရိက် *rĩk*, to curse. Over the အ *a*, whether written or inherent, it induces also a guttural sound as အက် *ãk*, yes; အံ *ãn*, to long for, to yearn after, မံ *mãn*, meat, ဂြံ *grãm*, to hasten, &c. In expressing it over the Roman character, I have adhered to its original form.

* See under head of Ascititious Powers, page 10.

Before proceeding further, it may be necessary to give the powers of the letters. I shall commence with ᰣ *a*, as being inherent after all the consonants, for the comprehension of the pronunciation of these latter, it is requisite that the powers of this vowel should be understood.

POWERS OF THE LETTERS.

ᰣ *A*

Is the basis of the vowels, and is inherent after all the consonants, when the latter are uncombined with any other vowel. It has the following sounds:

1. Of *e* in hen; as, ᰈᰰ *jan*, to be bad, ᰈᰯ *jal*, to have correct pronunciation, ᰑᰤᰰ *fyan*, a foeman, &c.

2. Of *u* in *rut;* as, ᰣᰯ *al*, new, fresh, ᰕᰳ *mat*, to blow (as fire), ᰕᰯ *mal*, to dibble, &c.

3. When succeeded by ᰭ the final *k*, or by ᰴ the *nyindó*, it takes the sound of *o* in mock, or in long; as, ᰕᰭ *mak*, a target, ᰜᰭ *lak*, to pour, ᰊᰓᰭ *tabak*, the stomach, ᰣᰏᰴ *áplang*, upon, ᰜᰴ *lang*, a stone, ᰣᰴᰅ ᰣᰴᰅ *ang nga ang nga*, bright, dazzling, &c.

When superscribed by ᰶ *ṛan*, it acquires a prolonged and guttural sound, see under the head of *Ṛan*, page 5.

In Roman characters it may be represented by *a*.

Pronunciation of the Consonants.

ᰀ Ka, is the first letter of the alphabet, equally with all the consonants when uncombined with any other vowels, it inherits ᰣ the short *a*. In writing the single consonants in Roman characters, I therefore affix this *a*.

ᰀ Ka, is sounded like its English equivalent K; as *ki*, cotton.

ᰁ Kha, the second letter, is the same as the above aspirated; as, *khui*, twenty.

ᰂ Ga, is the English hard G; as, *go*, I.

ᰃ Nga, a naso-guttural is sounded like the nge in singer; as, *nga la*, truly, evidently.

ᰄ Ch, is sounded as ch in chair; thus, *che*, to value, to have regard for.

ᰅ Chh, is the same as the above aspirated; as, *chho*, a book.

ᰆ Ja, is pronounced like the French *j*; thus, *ju*, a thorn.

ᰇ Nya, is a palatal ny, and is sounded as nea in near; thus, *nyo*, to be ominous.

ᰊ Ta, is like the English T; thus, *ti*, to be great.

ᰋ Tha, is an aspirated dento-palatal th; thus, *thi*, to arrive.

ᰌ Da, is the same as the English D; thus, *dú*, to be white.

ᰍ Na, is like the English N; thus, *ne*, a cave.

ᰎ Pa, like the English P; thus, *pi*, to write.

ᰏ Pha, a labial ph; thus, *phi*, to be late.

ᰐ Fa, like the English F; thus, *fá*, to swim.

ᰒ Ba, like the English B; thus, *bi*, vegetable.

ᰕ Ma, like the English M; thus, *mi*, fire.

ᰖ Tsa, is a palatal ts; thus, *tsun*, to bray, to pound.

ᰗ Tsh, the above aspirated; thus, *tsho*, colour.

ᰘ Za, as *z* in zenith;* thus, *ze*, gunpowder.

ᰚ Ya, as *y* in year; thus, *yá*, to perish, to become extinct.

ᰛ Ra, is like the English R;* thus, *ru*, a cane.

---

* See under head of Ascititious Powers, page 10.

ᰜ La, like the English L; thus, ᰜᰧ *li*, a house.

ᰝ Ha, like the English H; thus, ᰝᰦ *há*, wax.

ᰟ Va, as the English V; thus, ᰟᰦ *vá*, to vibrate.

ᰠ Sa, like the English S; thus, ᰠᰦ *sá*, to be clear, fair.

ᰡ Sha, same as the above aspirated; thus, ᰡᰧ *shi*, to see.

ᰢ Wa, should be pronounced with the *full rounded sound* of the English W;* thus, ᰢ *wa*, to be fit for, to be worthy of; as, ᰢᰨᰦᰖ *wómo*, a fox.

ᰁ Kla, is a palatal kl, sounded as cl in clear; thus, ᰁ *kla*, to cut through, or divide with one stroke.

ᰄ Gla, as gl in glow; thus, ᰄᰧ ᰜ *gli la*, distinctly.

ᰏ Pla, labial pl as in plan; thus, ᰏ *pla*, to issue out of.

ᰒ Fla, a dento-labial fl as in flat; thus, ᰒᰧ *fli*, to divide, to separate.

ᰔ Bla, a labial bl as in bland; thus, ᰔᰪ *blu*, a ridge.

ᰖ Mla, a labial ml; as, ᰖᰨ *mlo*, an article.

ᰞ Hla, a palatal hl; as, ᰞᰨ *hlo*, a high mountain.

Pronunciation of the Vowels.

ᰣ A, as already explained in page 6.

ᰣᰦ A′, has the long sound of a in far; as, ᰀᰰᰦ *kán*, to be excited, ᰓᰰᰦ *bán*, a knife, ᰎᰲᰦ *pár*, to buy. It bears also a short pronunciation, like the o in among, as, ᰈᰵᰦ *jáng* to be close (as basket work, &c.) (See remark with reference to this, under ᰶ *ran*, page 5.)

ᰣᰧ I, is pronounced as the Latin or Italian *i*. It has both a long and short accent, when bearing the former sound, it is distinguished by being sur-

* It is not pronounced so *generally* by the Lepchas, but should be taught so.

mounted by *ran*, thus, *li*, to speak, *lin bo*, a speaker, *ding*, to stand, *rit*, to distribute, *bik*, a cow, *bik*, to split or burst open, *mit*, a female, &c.

O has the sound of o in no, as: *ámo*, mother, *ábo*, father, *go*, I, &c.

The Lepchas are apt to pronounce this letter as *u*, and hence when writing, to confound it with *ú*, this error should be avoided, and corrected in the Lepchas.

O′, is the broad o, as, in nor, for, thus, *mór*, butter.

U, is a short close u pronounced somewhat like the French eu in lieu, jeu, thus, *zu*, to be striped; *bu*, a load.

U′, is a long broad u, as u in rule or oo in moon, thus: *rú*, to be old; *dú*, to dig; *núm*, a debt.

E is pronounced as the Latin e or the English short a in day, may; thus: *pe*, a pattern. It likewise takes the sound of the e in the French word mere; as, *jer*, gold, also as e in ten, thus, *len*, than, *ren*, since.

Pronunciation of the Finals.

The Finals with their pronunciations, are given in note 3, page 4. They bear the sound of the English letter as written opposite each Final, under the head of Powers. They have not the inherent *a* attached, and can only be used at the end of a word or syllable, thus: *bik*, a fowl, *num*, oil, *tuknól*, a snail, *kólpót*, a walnut, *róp*, to adhere; *rungnyit*, name of a river in Sikim (improperly pronounced by Europeans *Rungeet*).

The last two Finals *kang* and *nyindó* may be considered as one letter or sign. The ᰵ *kang* is never affixed to a consonant, unless accompanied by some vowel or other sign, as by the *Ran* or by the *curved sign in the nyindó*, which sign appears to be merely a vehicle for the ᰴ, ᰵ *kang*.

The word ᰉᰧᰴᰌᰨ *nyindó* is derived from ཉི་བ, *nyi wa*, the sun and ཟླ་བ *zla wa* the moon, from some fancied resemblance in form thereto.

The pronunciations of the affixed consonant signs ᰤ, ᰀᰤ *kya* and ᰥ ᰀᰥ *kra* have been shown under note 4, pages 4 and 5. Like the regular consonants they possess the inherent short *a* affixed. A few letters, however, sometimes bear

Ascititious Powers.

Thus :—

ᰀᰥ *KRA*, ᰝᰥ *HRA*, ᰛ *RA* and ᰈ *ZA*

Assume occasionally the following pronunciations :—

ᰀᰥ *Kra*, takes sometimes the sound as of a hard rolling tr, thus,

ᰀᰥᰫ *krú*, a ship, pronounced as if written *trú*.

ᰝᰥ *Hra*, sometimes is sounded like an aspirated tr, thus,

ᰝᰥᰧᰵ *hri*, a couch, pronounced as if written *thri*.

ᰛ *Ra*, this consonant takes sometimes the sound of dr, thus,

ᰛᰶ ᰛᰨ *rán ró* pronounced as if written *drán dró*.

ᰈ *Za*, in a few instances takes the sound of dz, or the pronunciation of what the Italians call their soft z, as in the words *mezzo*, *zanzara*, &c., thus, the word ᰈᰦᰮᰓᰫᰜᰧᰵ is pronounced as if spelt *dzám bú ling*.

But in no pure Lepcha word do these letters take these pronunciations : it is only in words derived from the Tibetan or some foreign source, that they are so sounded, thus, for instance, in the examples just given :

Krú, corresponds to the Tibetan གྲུ *gru*, a ship.

Hri, to ཁྲི *khri*, a couch.

Rán ró, accords with འདྲ་འདྲ *b dra b dra*, equal.

Zám bú ling, is the same as the Tibetan word འཛམ་བུ་གླིང *h dsam bu gling*, corresponding to the Sanscrit जम्बु द्वीप the central division of the earth.

I have introduced a sign (which the Lepchas, who have been taught it, have at once adopted) to render the letters when bearing these pronunciations easily distinguishable. A dot under the letter effects this, thus

Ḳra *Ḥra* *Ṛa* *Ẓa*

so the examples given, would be written

Ḳrú *Ḥri* *Ṛán ṛó* *Ẓám bú ling*

Lepchas sometimes give these pronunciations to words that ought not to possess them, the following of this error ought to be guarded against.

Gṛ. might have been advantageously introduced to represent གྲ *gr*, (hard sound) in words derived from the Tibetan, which are now spelt with *Kr*, or *R*, indefinitely. Not being, however, adopted by the Lepchas, I have not brought it into use.

PART II.

SYLLABIC SCHEME.

The following is a synopsis of the Letters, Vowels, and Finals combined, arranged in Alphabetical order, forming syllables, and comprehending all the forms that words in the Lepcha Language can take.

1.—*Vowels and Finals combined.*

a	ak	am	al	an	ap	ar	at	ang
ᰣ	ᰣᰭ	ᰣᰮ	ᰣᰯ	ᰣᰰ	ᰣᰱ	ᰣᰲ	ᰣᰳ	ᰣᰴ
ȃ	ȃk	ȃm	ȃl	ȃn	ȃp	ȃr	ȃt	ȃng
ᰣᰶ	ᰣᰶᰭ	ᰣᰶᰮ	ᰣᰶᰯ	ᰣᰶᰰ	ᰣᰶᰱ	ᰣᰶᰲ	ᰣᰶᰳ	ᰣᰶᰴ
á	ák	ám	ál	án	áp	ár	át	áng
ᰣᰦ	ᰣᰦᰭ	ᰣᰦᰮ	ᰣᰦᰯ	ᰣᰦᰰ	ᰣᰦᰱ	ᰣᰦᰲ	ᰣᰦᰳ	ᰣᰦᰴ
i	ik	im	il	in	ip	ir	it	ing
ᰣᰧ	ᰣᰧᰭ	ᰣᰧᰮ	ᰣᰧᰯ	ᰣᰧᰰ	ᰣᰧᰱ	ᰣᰧᰲ	ᰣᰧᰳ	ᰣᰧᰴ
ȋ	ȋk	ȋm	ȋl	ȋn	ȋp	ȋr	ȋt	ȋng
ᰣᰧᰶ	ᰣᰧᰶᰭ	ᰣᰧᰶᰮ	ᰣᰧᰶᰯ	ᰣᰧᰶᰰ	ᰣᰧᰶᰱ	ᰣᰧᰶᰲ	ᰣᰧᰶᰳ	ᰣᰧᰶᰴ
o	ok	om	ol	on	op	or	ot	ong
ᰣᰨ	ᰣᰨᰭ	ᰣᰨᰮ	ᰣᰨᰯ	ᰣᰨᰰ	ᰣᰨᰱ	ᰣᰨᰲ	ᰣᰨᰳ	ᰣᰨᰴ
ó	ók	óm	ól	ón	óp	ór	ót	óng
ᰣᰩ	ᰣᰩᰭ	ᰣᰩᰮ	ᰣᰩᰯ	ᰣᰩᰰ	ᰣᰩᰱ	ᰣᰩᰲ	ᰣᰩᰳ	ᰣᰩᰴ

u	uk	um	ul	un	up	ur	ut	ung
ú	úk	úm	úl	ún	úp	úr	út	úng
e	ek	em	el	en	ep	er	et	eng

2.—*Consonants with Vowels and Finals combined.*

ka	kak	kam	kal	kan	kap	kar	kat	kang
k͡a	k͡ak	k͡am	k͡al	k͡an	k͡ap	k͡ar	k͡at	k͡ang
ká	kák	kám	kál	kán	káp	kár	kát	káng
ki	kik	kim	kil	kin	kip	kir	kit	king
k͡i	k͡ik	k͡im	k͡il	k͡in	k͡ip	k͡ir	k͡it	k͡ing
ko	kok	kom	kol	kon	kop	kor	kot	kong
kó	kók	kóm	kól	kón	kóp	kór	kót	kóng

ku	kuk	kum	kul	kun	kup	kur	kut	kung
kú	kúk	kúm	kúl	kún	kúp	kúr	kút	kúng
ke	kek	kem	kel	ken	kep	ker	ket	keng

In like manner are combined, the Vowels and Finals to the remaining thirty-four Consonants.

3.— *Kya affixed to the Vowels, with Finals combined.*

aya	ayak	ayam	ayal	ayan	ayap	ayar	ayat	ayang
ȃya	ȃyak	ȃyam	ȃyal	ȃyan	ȃyap	ȃyar	ȃyat	ȃyang
ayá	ayák	ayám	ayál	ayán	ayáp	ayár	ayát	ayáng
ayi	ayik	ayim	ayil	ayin	ayip	ayir	ayit	aying
ȃyi	ȃyik	ȃyim	ȃyil	ȃyin	ȃyip	ȃyir	ȃyit	ȃying
ayo	ayok	ayom	ayol	ayon	ayop	ayor	ayot	ayong

ayó	ayók	ayóm	ayól	ayón	ayóp	ayór	ayót	ayóng
ayu	ayuk	ayum	ayul	ayun	ayup	ayur	ayut	ayung
ayú	ayúk	ayúm	ayúl	ayún	ayúp	ayúr	ayút	ayúng
aye	ayek	ayem	ayel	ayen	ayep	ayer	ayet	ayeng

4.— *Kya affixed to the Consonants, with Vowels and Finals combined.*

kya	kyak	kyam	kyal	kyan	kyap	kyar	kyat	kyang
k͡ya	k͡yak	k͡yam	k͡yal	k͡yan	k͡yap	k͡yar	k͡yat	k͡yang
kyá	kyák	kyám	kyál	kyán	kyáp	kyár	kyát	kyáng
kyi	kyik	kyim	kyil	kyin	kyip	kyir	kyit	kying
k͡yi	k͡yik	k͡yim	k͡yil	k͡yin	k͡yip	k͡yir	k͡yit	k͡ying
kyo	kyok	kyom	kyol	kyon	kyop	kyor	kyot	kyong
kyó	kyók	kyóm	kyól	kyón	kyóp	kyór	kyót	kyóng

kyu	kyuk	kyum	kyul	kyun	kyup	kyur	kyut	kyung
kyú	kyúk	kyúm	kyúl	kyún	kyúp	kyúr	kyút	kyúng
kye	kyek	kyem	kyel	kyen	kyep	kyer	kyet	kyeng

Similarly the Kya and the Finals, &c., are affixed to the remaining twenty-one Consonants. See page 4.

5.— *Kra affixed, with Vowels and Finals combined.*

kra	krak	kram	kral	kran	krap	krar	krat	krang
krā	krāk	krām	krāl	krān	krāp	krār	krāt	krāng
krá	kráh	krám	král	krán	kráp	krár	krát	kráng
kri	krik	krim	kril	krin	krip	krir	krit	kring
krī	krīk	krīm	krīl	krīn	krīp	krīr	krīt	krīng
kro	krok	krom	krol	kron	krop	kror	krot	krong

kró krók króm król krón króp krór krót króng

kru kruk krum krul krun krup krur krut krung

krú krúk krúm krúl krún krúp krúr krút krúng

kre krek krem krel kren krep krer kret kreng

And so on with the remaining seven letters (see page 5).

6.— *kya and* *kra united, and combined with Consonants, Vowels and Finals.*

krya kryak kryam kryal kryan kryap kryar kryat kryang

kry͡a kry͡ak kry͡am kry͡al kry͡an kry͡ap kry͡ar kry͡at kry͡ang

kryá kryák kryám kryál kryán kryáp kryár kryát kryáng

kryi kryik kryim kryil kryin kryip kryir kryit krying

kry͡i kry͡ik kry͡im kry͡il kry͡in kry͡ip kry͡ir kry͡it kry͡ing

kryo kryok kryom kryol kryon kryop kryor kryot kryong

kryó	kryók	kryóm	kryól	kryón	kryóp	kryór	kryót	kryóng
ᰀᰤᰥᰩ	ᰀᰤᰥᰩᰭ	ᰀᰤᰥᰩᰮ	ᰀᰤᰥᰩᰯ	ᰀᰤᰥᰩᰰ	ᰀᰤᰥᰩᰱ	ᰀᰤᰥᰩᰲ	ᰀᰤᰥᰩᰳ	ᰀᰤᰥᰩᰵ
kryu	kryuk	kryum	kryul	kryun	kryup	kryur	kryut	kryung
ᰀᰤᰥᰪ	ᰀᰤᰥᰪᰭ	ᰀᰤᰥᰪᰮ	ᰀᰤᰥᰪᰯ	ᰀᰤᰥᰪᰰ	ᰀᰤᰥᰪᰱ	ᰀᰤᰥᰪᰲ	ᰀᰤᰥᰪᰳ	ᰀᰤᰥᰪᰵ
kryú	kryúk	kryúm	kryúl	kryún	kryúp	kryúr	kryút	kryúng
ᰀᰤᰥᰫ	ᰀᰤᰥᰫᰭ	ᰀᰤᰥᰫᰮ	ᰀᰤᰥᰫᰯ	ᰀᰤᰥᰫᰰ	ᰀᰤᰥᰫᰱ	ᰀᰤᰥᰫᰲ	ᰀᰤᰥᰫᰳ	ᰀᰤᰥᰫᰵ
krye	kryek	kryem	kryel	kryen	kryep	kryer	kryet	kryeng
ᰀᰤᰥᰬ	ᰀᰤᰥᰬᰭ	ᰀᰤᰥᰬᰮ	ᰀᰤᰥᰬᰯ	ᰀᰤᰥᰬᰰ	ᰀᰤᰥᰬᰱ	ᰀᰤᰥᰬᰲ	ᰀᰤᰥᰬᰳ	ᰀᰤᰥᰬᰵ

In like manner are the remaining seven letters written.*

In this scheme may be seen every form that words of one syllable can take. If each letter be carried out, with the vowels and finals affixed, it will give 7,290 monosyllabic words.

The Lepcha Language is essentially a monosyllabic language, for though it has words of more than one syllable, these are words which are formed by compounds of two different words; or by the same word reduplicated, or connected by an epenthesis; or by certain prefixed syllables common to many words, as, ᰊᰪᰭ *tuk*, ᰊᰪᰵ *tung*, ᰜᰪᰭ *luk*, ᰎᰪᰰ *pun*, &c., which may be abscindable or inabscindable; commutable or immutable; according to the nature of the word. By the addition of these particles, the sense of the word may be completely altered, or may remain unchanged; may be slightly modified, or may be transmuted from verb to substantive or to adjective; but the word itself retains the radical form of its syllable as laid down in this scheme.

---

* The Lepchas when writing, used generally to affix the ᰥ *kra* to the ᰤ *kya* as a more speedy mode of writing, and so it will be found in their manuscripts, thus—ᰀᰥᰤ for ᰀᰤᰥ *krya*.

The following are examples of,

DISSYLLABLES.

7.—*Compounded of two words.*

kóng-yóng, independence, (from སྐང *skang*, the foot; and ཡང *yang*, light, light-footed, free).

lák-chhó, a tool, an instrument, (from ལག *lag* the hand; and ཆ *chha* an article).

phák-zu, a brush, (from ཕག *phag*, a hog, a pig; and ཟེད *zed*, a bristle).

ngan-she, fore-knowledge, (from སྔོན་པ *sngon pa*, before former; and ཤེས་པར *shes par*, to know).

sák-dak, to be sorry, to be grieved, (from *sák*, the mind, or its state, [in compos]; and *dak*, to be in pain).

tám-blyók, a butterfly, (from *thám*, a thing; and *blyók*, to be unsubstantial, incorporeal), &c.

8.—*Formed by reduplication, or connected by an epenthesis.*

dun dun. }
dun-na dun-na } drizzling (rain).

dúr-ra dúr-ra, full flowing, flaunting (robes).

hryáp-pa hryop-pa, loose, ricketty.

lák-ka lok-ka, unstable, fickle, versatile.

jin-na jin-na, twinkling (as star), &c.

9.—*Formed by prefixed Particles or Syllables common to many words.*

ABSCINDABLE.

á-ka or *ka*, the hand.

á-fo ,, *fo*, a tooth.

á-thyák ,, *thyák*, the head

á-dyáng or *dyáng*, the leg.

sa-tsuk ,, *tsuk*, the sun.

ta-só ,, *só*, yesterday.

10.—*Inabscindable.*

ka-jú, a dog.

kum-dúng, another.

la-háp, a recess.

luk-ayeng, fetid.

mun-jú, awkward.

na-vár, a boat.

pa-lit, a flute.

pur-ayám, a mole.

pa-no, king.

ruk-nyám, prevarication.

sa-dyar, a thunderbolt.

sa-hór, a star.

suk-vyar, mud.

sung-hlyo, a spear.

tuk-po, string, cord, &c.

ka-tá, single, alone.

kur-thák, a king's minister.

la-vo, the moon.

ma-ri, dirt.

mung-kyek, forked lightning.

num-prúm, an old woman.

pá-ku, a reticule.

ra-kú, a store.

mung-yúng, a pea-fowl.

sa-gór, a cliff.

sa-nóng, snow.

sum-pyar, tail of fish.

ta-lyáng, the sky.

tung-kúng, a rainbow.

11.—*Commutable.*

kum-byong, or *pum-byong*, a cloud.

kum-thyóng, ,, *pun-thyóng*, a kite (bird).

tuk-mo, ,, *kut-mo*, theft.

pun-nyóm, ,, *put-nyóm*, an old man.

sa-nyi, ,, *suk-nyi*, the day.

sa-fyum, ,, *pur-fyum*, a breeze.

But of the abscindable and commutable, the instances are comparatively not numerous. With the exception of the ᰣᰦ *á* particle, few of the prefixes can be dropped, and not many changed, without altering the sense of the word.

If the order of this scheme be carried out to its full, with the syllables prefixed to each word, it will give the large number of 53,144,100 words, dissyllables alone, all of which, (though they do not really exist), may be expressed in the Lepcha language.

12.—TRISYLLABLES.

With the exceptions of the words to which the adjective and adverbial particles ᰓᰨ *bo*, and ᰜ *la*, are affixed, there are only three or four Trisyllabic words in the Lepcha language; the following are examples,

ᰍᰪᰮ ᰡᰧᰮ ᰉᰨ *num-shim-nyo*, a man, human being.

ᰍᰪᰵ ᰜᰤᰬᰰ ᰍᰨ *nung-lyen-no*, the guardian spirit of males.

ᰀ ᰋᰵ ᰑᰧ *ka-thang-fi*, the guardian spirit of females.

The first, ᰍᰪᰮ ᰡᰧᰮ ᰉᰨ *num-shim-nyo*, is compounded of ᰍᰪᰮ *num*, one of the prefixed particles (here abscindable), common to many words, (the letters implying, a created thing); of ᰡᰧᰮ *shim*, a being, (from ᰡᰧ *shi*, to be); and ᰉᰨ *nyo*, a female, (literally proceeding from). The derivation of the latter words are more complex; the former of the two implies, the leader to ᰍᰦᰵ *náng*, (literally, straight-forwardness) sincerity. The latter signifies, the controller of (causing to fear) the will.

13.—POLYSYLLABLES.

There are none.

PART III.

THE PARTS OF SPEECH.

Formative.—Etymology.

Equally with the Occidental languages, the Lepcha language may be divided into

Article, ...	*blang-jak.*
Noun, ...	*á-blang.*
Adjective, ...	*blang-gyú.*
Pronoun, ...	*blang-lam.*
Verb, ...	*á-shóp.*
Adverb, ...	*shóp-gyú.*
Preposition, or Postposition, ...	*blang-hyop.*
Conjunction, ...	*ring-shok.*
Interjection, ...	*ring ta-lo.*
also	
Verbal particles, ...	*shóp-hyop.**

Of which we will severally treat.

---

* Grammatical or Scientific terms do not form part of a primitive language: they are the offspring of cultivation. I introduce the above, as appropriate equivalents of the English words; I do not in this work carry out this neological system, but I may hereafter compose a Grammar in Lepcha, (for the benefit of the Lepchas), in which all Grammatical terms will be inserted.

1st.—*Of the Articles.*

The English Indefinite Article, "*a*," or "*an*," is not ordinarily made use of in the Lepcha, but when it is employed, it is expressed by, *kát*, one, as, *fa-lyeng kát*, a young man, *wó-mo kát vóng ká muk*, a fox crept into a thicket.

The Definite Article "*the*," is represented by, *re*, as, *pa-no re*, the king, *chho re*, the book.

re, bears also an inflected form, and then becomes, *rem*, as, *hu pa-no rem shú*, he petitioned the king.

Another form, but less definite than, *re*, for expressing the Article, "the," is denoted by as, *ma-ró mu li*, the person said. But it is seldom if ever, unless preceded by a stated number, affixed to the governing noun, thus, *kát mu kát ká li*, the one said to the other, *ma-ró nyat mu lyáng kor lung lóm*, the two men travelled round the country.

It is, however, in its oblique form, and in its office of showing distinction between the governing and governed nouns, that *mu*, is more particularly serviceable. It then changes to , and in this form may directly follow the noun, and may be used definitely or indefinitely, thus, *kát mu kát mum li*, the one said to the other, *hu tung-hóng mum klo*, he fell into the hole, *to sa-re Ta-she mum den ri sho*, whosoever shall believe in Tashe.

2nd.—Of Nouns.

Substantive nouns are expressed by simple words representing the thing, thus, *fat*, earth; *suk-dum*, the earth, world; *ta-lyáng*, the heavens, &c. Abstract and other formative nouns, will be hereafter discussed.

3rd.—Of Gender.

Gender is confined to living beings, male and female, and words are uninflected by either masculine or feminine. There is no expressed Neuter. Hence, strictly speaking, nouns are, in the Lepcha language, without gender.

The terms to express the gender of human beings, are different from those used to indicate the gender of inferior animals.

The male of human beings is distinguished by *ta-gri*; the female is denoted by *ta-ayu.*

These follow the rule of adjectives, and succeed the substantive, thus, *ma-ró*, a person, *ma-ró ta-gri*, a male person, *ma-ró ta-ayu*, a female person.

They may also be used substantively, as, *hu ta-gri gum*, he is a male, *hu ta-ayu gum*, she is a female, *ta-gri kup*, a little male, *ta-ayu kup*, a little female; but they are of course still adjectives, substantives in these cases being always understood.

The distinction between sexes of animals, inferior to man, is expressed, the male by *á-bu*, the female by *á-mót.* These, likewise, follow the substantive, and like almost all adjectives, commencing with *á*, when affixed to a noun, may, (and here euphonically do) drop the *á*, thus, *hik*, a fowl, *hik bu*, a cock, *hik mot*, a hen; *on*, a horse, *on bu*, a stallion, *on mót*, a mare.

á-bu and *á-mót* are sometimes affixed, emphatically, to the terms for the male and female of human beings; thus, *ta-grĭ bu*, a male (person); *ta-ayu mót*, a female (person).

The males of some few animals, as of goats and pigs, are expressed by *á-tsu*; as, *luk*, a sheep, *luk tsu*, a ram; *món*, a pig, *món tsu*, a boar; *sa-ár*, a goat, *sa-ár tsu*, a male goat.

A term *lóng*, (Tibetan གླང *glang*, a bull), is used to denote the males of some large animals; as *bik*, a cow, *bik lóng*, a bull; *sung-vo*, a buffaloe, *sung-vo lóng*, a male buffaloe; *sa-ving*, large deer (cervus elephas), *sa-ving lóng*, a stag; *tyáng-mo*, an elephant, *tyáng-mo lóng*, a male elephant; *sa-lók*, a rhinoceros, *sa-lók lóng*, a male rhinoceros.

The female term in contradistinction both to *á-tsu*, and *lóng*, is *á-mót*.

mĭt, a female, is also affixed to express the gender of superior beings; thus, *rum*, a good spirit, a god, *rum-mĭt*, a goddess; *yet tung-kúng mĭt*, a water goddess; *tung-kúng tung-lá mĭt*, nymphs and syrens. Like *á-mót*, it is sometimes emphatically added to the ordinary gender term; so, *ta-ayu mĭt*, a female, a woman.

There are some words which in themselves express the sex of the person, without the aid of any gender term; thus—with regard to relationship,

á-bo, *á-mo*, father, mother; *á-num*, an elder brother; *á-nóm*, an elder sister, (not so with the younger, here the usual terms would be affixed; thus, *ayeng*, a child, a younger [brother or sister], *ayeng ta-grĭ*, a younger brother, *ayeng ta-ayu*, a younger sister); *á-kú*, a paternal uncle; *á-jóng*, a maternal uncle; *á-nyú*, an aunt; *á-fyat*, a father-in-law; *myók*, a son-in-law; *nyóm*, a daughter-in-law; *á-zóng*, a (yonnger) brother-in-law; *á-ngóp*, a (younger) sister-in-law; *mo sung-mo*, a female cousin, &c.

Likewise, in connection with age, the sex is rendered manifest; thus, *fa-lyeng*, a young man; *num-lyeng*, a young woman; *mo-nang*, an elderly woman; *pa-nyóm*, an old man; *num-prúm*, an old woman. *pa-nyóm*, and *num-prúm*, are sometimes, in familiar language, applied to beasts; thus, *bik num-prúm ngún nón*, the cow has become old, (an old woman).

So also with respect to rank; *pa-no*, a king; *pun-di*, a queen; *á-thing*, a lord, master; *á-nyo*, a lady; a gentle-woman, &c.

The term *á-lyeng*, is applied to any young *female*,* rising to maturity; thus, *bik*, a cow, *bik lyeng*, a young matured cow, that has not borne young; *sa-ár lyeng*, a young female goat; *hik lyeng*, a young hen; *fo lyeng*, a young female bird, &c.

á-mi is applied to a young (or until it has had young) female pig; thus, *món mi*, a sow, (that has not had young).

á-gú is a word implying maturity in female beasts, (having borne young); thus, *bik gú*, a matured cow; *món gú*, a matured sow; *sung-vo gú*, a matured female buffaloe, &c..

---

* *á-lyeng*, is applicable only to females; the word *fa-lyeng*, a young man, is exceptional, and may be considered a distinct word. *num-lyeng*, a young woman, may be likewise so considered; neither *fa*, nor *num*, has a separate signification, each being merely one of the prefixed particles, common to many words. Both words, however, obviously take their root from *á-lyeng*.

á-bom is applied to female fowls and birds, that have arrived at maturity (season of incubation), thus, *hik bom*, a matured hen; *fo bom*, a matured female bird.

There are other words betokening qualities in sexes, consequently indicating the gender, thus, *a-tang* denotes a corpulent male beast, as, *ka-jú tang*, a corpulent male dog; *món tang*, a bulky boar, &c.

á-bo is applied to an entire (non-emasculated) male beast, as, *món bo*, a boar; *on bo*, a stallion, &c.

4.—*Of Numbers.*

There are three numbers, *viz.*, Singular, Dual, and Plural. The Singular may be represented by the simple noun. The Dual is expressed by affixing to the noun, the word *nyum*. And the Plural by affixing *sang* or *pang*, thus—

ma-ró, or *ma-ró kát*, a person.

ma-ró nyum, two persons.

ma-ró sang, persons.

The difference between the two plural terms, is, *sang*, is applied chiefly to hman beings; *pang*, to inferior animals, and to inanimate things.

pang, may, however, be made to denote the plural of human, or inferior beings, and of inanimate things, indifferently. *sang*, although it may be applied to all living animals, human or inferior, can never be correctly affixed as a plural sign to inanimate things; thus,

ma-ró sang, or *ma-ró pang*, people.

bik pang, or *bik sang*, cows.

li pang, (never *li sang*,) houses.

These terms may be affixed to the pronoun, independently of the noun, or may sometimes stand in room of the noun, thus—

á-re sang, these people, or animals.

o-re pang, those things, animals, or people.

sa-kon sang, Sakons, *i. e.*, Sakon and his people or companions.

5.—*Of Declension of Nouns.*

Substantive nouns being uninflected by Cases, the latter may, be said to, be limited to the Nominative and Objective.

There are, however, certain post-positive particles which may be used to form a full Declension, thus—

The Nominative is represented by the simple noun, or if the word be in the Singular number and indefinite, *kát*, one, a, or an, may be added to the noun; if definite, the particle *re*, the, may be, either in the singular or plural, affixed.

The Instrumental, is formed by affixing to the Nominative, the particle *nun*.

The Dative is denoted by the post-position *ká*.

The Accusative may be distinguished by affixing to the noun, when definite or indefinite, the particle *mum*, and when definite the particle *rem*. (See under head of Articles, page 23).

The Vocative is indicated by the prepositive particle *e*, and, if the final letter of the word be a vowel by affixing, *á*, or *wá*. If the word end with a consonant, the final is re-duplicated in the particles, thus—

e á bo á, or *e á-bo wá*, O Father, *e á-kup pá*, O child.

But either the preposition or the post-position may be, at pleasure, dropped, thus, *e a-bo,* O father, *á-kup pa,* O child.

The following is an example of a noun so declined.

pa-no, a king.

SINGULAR.

Nom. *pa-no,* a king.

Inst. *pa-no nun,* a king, by a king.

Gen. *pa-no sa,* of a king, a king's.

Dat. *pa-no ká,* to a king.

Acc. *pa-no mum,* a, or the king.

Voc. *e pa-no wá,* O king.

Abl. *pa-no nun,* from a king.

DUAL.

Nom. *pa-no nyum,* two kings.

Inst. *pa-no nyum nun,* two kings, by two kings.

Gen. *pa-no nyum sa,* of two kings.

Dat. *pa-no nyum ká,* to two kings.

Acc. *pa-no nyum mum,* two kings.

Voc. *e pa-no nyum má,* O two kings.

Abl. *pa-no nyum nun,* from two kings.

PLURAL.

Nom. *pa-no sang,* kings.

Inst. *pa-no sang nun,* kings, by kings.

Gen. *pá-no sang sa,* of kings.

Dat. *pa-no sang ká,* to kings.

Acc. *pa-no sang mum*, kings.
Voc. *e pa-no sang ngá*, O kings.
Abl. *pa-no sang nun*, from kings.

In like manner, all Substantive nouns may be declined.

6.—*Of Adjectives.*

Adjectives are primitive or compositive. The latter may be formed from verbs by, in many instances, conjoining to the verb, *á*, by prosthesis, thus—

VERB.	ADJECTIVE.
chór, to be sour.	*á-chór*, sour.
krúp, to be astringent.	*á-krúp*, astringent.
klyám, to be sweet.	*á-klyám*, sweet.
klyom, to be insipid.	*á-klyom*, insipid.
náng, to be straight.	*á-náng*, straight.
kol, to be crooked.	*á-kol*, crooked.
hyang, to be cold.	*á-hyang*, cold.
kyang, to be light (not heavy).	*á-kyang*, light.
nók, to be black.	*á-nók*, black.

When the verb ends in a vowel, the adjective generally assumes a final m; as,

ryú, to be good.	*á-ryúm*, good.
kri, to be bitter.	*á-krim*, bitter.
li, to be heavy.	*á-lim*, heavy.
dú, to be white.	*á-dúm*, white.
ti, to be large.	*á-tim*, large.

chu, to be small.	*á-chum*, small.
shú, to be fat.	*á-shúm*, fat, corpulent.
hrú, to be hot.	*á-hrúm*, hot.
zú, to be alive.	*á-zúm*, alive, living.

But all do not acquire this additional particle, for instance.

rú, to be old.	*á-rú*, old.
hlu, to be languid.	*á-hlu*, languid.
má, to be secret.	*á-má*, secret.
hlyá, to be unctuous.	*á-hlyá*, unctuous.

The two latter formations however, are, not numerous, the examples given being nearly all that could be cited.

The assumption of the paragogic *m*, has, doubtless for its cause, a regard to euphony, but the rejection of it in homologous words, without any apparent reason, (for the adoption of it in the rejected cases, would occasion no inconsonance), seems anomalous.

It may be remarked that all adjectives, derived from verbs whose final is a vowel, if they do take a final consonant, it is always the final *m*.

kur-dang, ruddy, blooming; and *kum-dúng*, another, are examples of primitive adjectives, derived from no verb, and having no adjective particle affixed. Other formations of adjectives, primitive and derivative, will be hereafter shown.

Adjectives, as a rule, follow the substantives, as, *on á-dúm* a white horse. They may be declined in the same manner, as described under head of declension of nouns; thus,

Singular.

Nom. *ma-ró á-ryúm*, a good person.

Gen. *ma-ró á-ryúm sa*, of a good person, &c.

Dual.

Dat. *ma-ró á-ryúm nyum ká*, to two good persons.

Acc. *ma-ró á-ryúm nyum mum*, two good persons, &c.

Plural.

Voc. *e ma-ró á-ryúm sang ngá*, O good people.

Abl. and Inst. *ma-ró á-ryúm sang nun*, from, by good people.

7.—*Of Degrees of Comparison.*

Comparative.

The Comparative degree is expressed by the comparative conjunction *len*, than. This is placed after the noun, (substantive, adjective, pronoun or verb) with which comparison is made; thus, *thám-chang len num-shim-nyo tĩ gum*, man is greater than the beasts, (literally, the beasts than, man great is); *á-re len o-re ryú*, that is better than this, (lit. this than, that good [is]); *hryóp len thyan ryú*, it is better to laugh, than to cry, (lit. to cry than, to laugh good [is]).

Superlative.

The Superlative degree is formed by comprising a totality, and then drawing comparison; thus, *hu gun len ryú*, he is the best, (lit. he all than, [is] good); *o-re gun len á-chum gum*, that is the least (lit. that all than, small is).

The Superlative may also be formed, by affixing to the root of the adjective, the word *chho*; thus, *á-tim*, great, *tim chho*, the greatest;

hu tĩm chho gum, he is the greatest. (This word *chho*, corresponds to the Tibetan མཆོག *mchhog*, the chief, the best).

When the signification is distinct, the signs of comparison need merely be understood, thus *á-re nyum ká sa-re ryú*, of these two, which is good, *i. e.*, better, *á-yú nóng ká to tĩ gum*, who among you is great, *i. e.*, the greatest.

8.—*Of Pronouns.*

Pronouns, like Substantive nouns, have three numbers, *viz.*, Singular, Dual and Plural. The words, representing the Personal Pronouns, differ in each of the numbers, they also bear inflection in the Objective case, and may be declined similarly to substantives, as follows:

PERSONAL PRONOUNS.

1st Person.

go, I.

Singular.

Nom. *go*, I.	Dat. *ka-su ká*, to me.
Inst. *go nun*, I, by me.	Acc. *ka-sum*, me.
Gen. *ka-su*, of me, my.	Abl. *ka-su nun*, from me.

Dual.

Nom. *ka-nyĩ*, we two	Acc. *ka-nyĩm*, or *ka-nyum*, us two.
Inst. *ka-nyĩ nun*, we two.	
Gen. *ka-nyĩ sa*, of us two.	
Dat. *ka-nyĩ ká*, to us two.	Abl. *ka-nyĩ nun*, from us two.

Plural.

Nom. *ka-yú*, we.*

Inst. *ka-yú nun*, we, by us.

Gen. *ka-yú sa*, of us, our's.

Dat. *ka-yú ká*, to us.

Acc. *ka-yúm*, us.

Abl. *ka-yú nun*, from us.

2nd Person.

hó, thou.

Singular.

Nom. *hó*, thou.

Inst. *hó nun*, thou, by thee.

Gen. *hó sa*, of thee, thy.

Dat. *hó ká*, to thee.

Acc. *hó mum*, thee.

Voc. *e hó*, O thou.

Abl. *hó nun*, from thee.

Dual.

Nom. *a-nyi*, you two.

Inst. *á-nyi nun*, you two.

Gen. *á-nyi sa*, of you two.

Dat. *á-nyi ká*, to you two.

Acc. *á-nyim*, *á-nyum*, } you two.

Voc. *e á-nyi*, O you two.

Abl. *á-nyi nun*, from you two.

Plural.

Nom. *á-yú*, you, or ye.

Inst. *á-yú nun*, you, by you.

Gen. *á-yú sa*, of you, your.

Dat. *á-yú ká*, to you.

Acc. *á-yúm*, you, or ye.

Voc. *e á-yú*, O you, O ye.

Abl. *á-yú nun*, from you.

---

* See also remark on *ká-yú*, and *ká*, p. 40.

The radical form was sometimes inelegantly used in the Dual, and Plural, thus, *hó-nyi*, for *á-nyi*; *hó-yú*, for *á-yú*, but this form would be rarely met with now.

3rd Person.

hu, he, she, or it.

Singular.

Nom. *hu*, he, she, or it.	Dat. *hu ká*, to him, her, or it.
Inst. *hu nun*, he, she, or it.	Acc. *hum*, him, her, or it.
Gen. *hu sa*, of him, her, or it; his, her's, or its.	Abl. *hu nun*, from him, her, or it.

Dual.

Nom. *hu-nyi*, they two.	Acc. *hu-nyim*, *hu-nyum*, } them (two).
Inst. *hu-nyi nun*, they two.	Abl. *hu-nyi nun*, from them two.
Gen. *hu-nyi sa*, of them (two).	
Dat. *hu-nyi ká*, to them (two).	

Plural.

Nom. *hu-yú*, they.	Dat. *hu-yú ká*, to them.
Inst. *hu-yú nun*, they.	Acc. *hu-yúm*, them.
Gen. *hu-yú sa*, of them.	Abl. *hu-yú nun*, from them.

Possessive Pronouns

May be formed from the Genitive of the Personal, thus,

1st Person.

Singular.

Nom. *ka-su*, my, mine.

Inst. *ka su nun*, my, by my.

Gen. *ka su sa*, of my, of mine.

Dat. *ka su sa ka*, to my, to mine.

Acc. *ka su sa mum*, my, mine.

Abl. *ka su sa nun*, from my, from mine.

In like manner the particles of Declension may be affixed to the Dual and Plural, *ka-nyi sa*, our two, *ka-yú sa*, our: also to the three Numbers of each of the 2nd and 3rd Persons, *hó sa*, thy, thine, *á-nyi sa*, your (two), *á-yú sa*, your, *hu sa*, his, her, or it's, *hu-nyi sa*, their (two), *hu-yú sa*, their.

Reciprocal Pronouns.

Corresponding to the English Pronouns compounded of self, are formed by the emphatic particle *do*. They may be thus declined,

1st Person.

Singular.

Nom. *ka-do*, I myself.

Inst. *ka-do nun*, I myself, by myself.

Gen. *ka-do sa*, *ka-do su*, of myself.

Dat. *ka-do ká*, to myself.

Acc. *ka-dom*, *ka-do mum*, myself.

Abl. *ka-do nun*, from myself.

Dual.

Nom. *ka-nyi do*, we two selves, we two ourselves.

Inst. *ka-nyi do nun*, we two selves, by our two selves.

Gen. *ka-nyi do sa*, of our two selves.

Dat. *ka-nyi do ká*, to our two selves.

Acc. { *ka-nyi dom,* / *ka-nyi do mum,* } our two selves.

Abl. *ka-nyi do nun*, from our two selves.

Plural.

Nom. *ka-yú do*, we ourselves.

Inst. *ka-yú do nun*, we ourselves, by ourselves.

Gen. *ka-yú do sa*, of ourselves.

Dat. *ka-yú do ká*, to ourselves.

Acc. { *ka-yú dom,* / *ka-yú do mum.* } ourselves.

Abl. *ka-yú do nun*, from ourselves.

2nd Person.

á-do,
or
hó do,
} thou thyself.

Singular.

Nom. *á-do*, thou thyself.

Inst. *á-do nun*, thou thyself, by thyself.

Gen. *á-do sa*, of thyself.

Dat. *á-do ká*, to thyself.

Acc. { *á-dom,* / *á-do mum,* } thyself.

Abl. *á-do nun*, from thyself.

In like manner may be declined, the Dual and Plural, also the 2nd and 3rd persons, thus—

Dual.

Nom. *á-nyi do*, your two selves, you two yourselves.

Obj. { *á-nyi dom*, / *á-nyi do mum.* } your two selves.

Plural.

Nom. *á-yú do*, you yourselves.

Obj. { *á-yú dom*, / *á-yú do mum*, } yourselves.

3rd Person.

Singular.

Nom. *hu do*, he himself, his self.

Obj. { *hu dom*, / *hu do mum*, } himself.

Dual.

Nom. *hu-nyi do*, they two themselves.

Obj. { *hu-nyi dom*, / *hu-nyi do mum*, } their two selves. / them (two) selves.

Plural.

Nom. *hu-yú do*, they themselves.

Obj. { *hu-yú dom*, / *hu-yu do mum*, } themselves, &c.

Emphatic Possessive Pronouns

Compounded of own, are formed from the Genitive of the Reciprocal, and may be declined in the usual manner, thus—

1st Person.

ka-do su, } my own.
ka-do sa, }

Singular.

Nom. *ka-do su*, my own.

Inst. *ka-do su nun*, my own, by my own.

Gen. *ka-do su sa*, of my own.

Dat. *ka-do su ká*, to my own.

Acc. { *ka-do sum*, } my own.
{ *ka-do su mum*, }

Abl. *ka-do su nun*, from my own.

And so may be declined the Dual and Plural and 2nd and 3rd Persons, as,

Dual.

Nom. *ka-nỹi do su*, our two own.

Gen. *ka-nỹi do su sa*, of our two own, &c.

Plural.

Nom. *ka-yú do su*, our own.

Obj. { *ka-yú do sum*, } our own.
{ *ka-yú do su mum*, }

2nd Person.

Singular.	Dual.
á-do su, thy own.	*á-nyi do su*, your two own

Plural.

á-yú do su, your own.

3rd Person.

Singular.

hu do su, his, her, it's own.

Dual.	Plural.
hu-nyi do su, their two own.	*hu-yú do su*, their own.

To the above the Particles of declension may be affixed when required.

ka-yú, the 1st person plural of the Personal Pronouns may be spelt *ká-yú*, which becomes converted by apocope to *ká*. This, *ká*, is more frequently used in the Nominative, Instrumental, Genitive, (or Possessive), and Ablative cases, it is seldom employed in the two other Objective cases, for instance, the Dative *ká ká*, is altogether cacophonous. The Accusative *kám*, though formerly very generally used, has become obsolete. *kám*, means, "a little," therefore, *kám bo*, would express, "give a little;" few Lepchas would now understand it to imply, "give us;" *ká mum*, however, is still quite intelligible. The emphatic Particle, *do*, is also affixed to, *ká*.

ka-yú is used in a general sense, and refers to a limited, or unlimited number; *ká*, is more definite and usually denotes the number to be limited or special, thus, *ka-yú gun na á-ryúm sang mum gó*, we all love the good, *ka-yú rum á-ryúm nyi yang ya*, we know that God is good, *ká sám nun ryúm bo nyi shang ká, ká do sa mát pang gyum lung ngak ka le.* Let we (us) three, that we may be good, be guardful of our acts, *ká num-shim-nyo thám-chang thám-bik re zang gum,* we, human beings, are but as the creatures of the earth, *a'r nun mát bá ka-yú nun ka-yú sa sák-chin rum kón tál la ching kón gát,* therefore, we should constrain our thoughts to aspire heaven-wards.

The 3rd Person, dual and plural of the personal, consequently, also of the Possesive, and Reciprocal Pronouns, including the singular number of the latter are frequently elided by syncope, and are written *ha-nyi,* for *hu-nyi;* *ha-yú,* for *hu yú;* *ha-do,* for *hu do,* &c.

hó do, the 2nd Person singular of the Reciprocal Pronouns, is usually used, when it is required to give particular emphasis to the person, thus, *hó do gum,* it is thou thyself, thou art the very person, *hó do zúk ka,* do it thyself.

á-do bears less significance, and is generally used in the objective case. It is also, by enallage, employed for the corresponding persons and numbers of the Personal and Possessive Pronouns, for instance, the following sentences would be rendered, *go á-dom bo sho,* for *go hó mum bo sho,* I will give thee; *á-do chho bu di,* for *hó sa chho bu di,* bring thy book. *á-do li pok nón,* for *hó sa li pok nón,* thy house has fallen, &c.

Among the Pronouns, it is only in these persons and numbers, that such commutations take place. The other persons and numbers, are used in their simple forms, thus, *hu á-nyum bo sho,* he will give you (two), *hu-yú á-yúm dun bo sho,* they will tell you, *hu sa on til nón,* his horse has fallen, *á-yú sa thi-kúng nyi -kúng,* your ancestors.

The inflected form *ka-sum*, *á-dom*, &c, may be considered, as the Particle *mum*, abbreviated and embodied in the Pronoun, thus, *hum*, instead of *hu mum*, &c.

Relative and Interrogative Pronouns.

The Pronouns, who, which and what, are severally expressed by *to*, *sa-re*, and *shu*.

As the Old English, who, and which, were formerly used for either persons or things, so in Lepcha, the *to*, and *sa-re*, are sometimes applied indiscriminately, thus, *sung-mut pum-byóng to chóng ngung a*, the clouds or the winds, who (for *sa-re*, which,) is the swifter, but the intermutation of these terms may be considered heterocletical. The distinction between *to* and *sa-re*, may be assumed to be the same as that which is at present observed between the English, who and which, or similar to the difference between the number signs, *sang*, and *pang*. *sa-re*, may be applied to things, animate or inanimate ; *to*, can only be applied correctly to persons.

The above Pronouns, may be declined, the same as Substantives, thus.

to, who.

Singular.

Nom. *to*, who.	Dat. *to ká*, to whom.
Inst. *to nun*, who, by whom.	Acc. *to mum*, whom.
Gen. *to sa*, of whom, whose.	Abl. *to nun*, from whom.

To this the Dual and Plural signs, and Particles of Declension may, when necessary be affixed, as, *go nun to nyum ká byi sho*, to whom (two) I shall give it, *to sang mát gang*, if any persons do it.

to, who, and *sa-re*, which, are both Relative and Interrogative. *shú*, what, is almost confined to the Interrogative, thus, *má-ró to nun zúk re*, the person who did it; *to nun klóng a*, who sent it? *ring sa-re go nun á-yúm ku ma*, the words which I have impressed upon you. *á-re nyum ká sa-re dóm sho*, of these two which will you select?

shú thám, what thing, *shú mát tung gó*, what are you doing? *shú gát shang a*, what do you want?

The Demonstrative Pronouns.

á-re, this, and *o-re*, that, may be declined the same way as the Relative Pronouns, thus,

á-re, this.

á-re nyum, these two.

á-re sang, these persons.

á-re pang, these people or things.

o-re, those.

o-re nyum, those two.

o-re sang, those persons.

o-re pang, those persons or things.

To these, the Emphatic Particle *do*, may be added, thus,

á-re do, this very.

á-re do nyum, these very two.

á-re do sang, these very persons.

o-re do, that very.

o-re do. nyum, those very two.

o-re do pang, those very things.

To all of the above, the Particles of declension may be affixed, as also to

The Pronominal Adjectives, and Adverbial Pronouns.

sa-tet, how much, how many, *á-tet*, this much, *o-tet*, that much, *ta-do*, one's own, *ma-ró do*, one's self, itself. Likewise to

---

The Distributive and Indefinite Pronouns.

re re, each, *gun*, all, every, *á-flik*, some, *kum-dúng*, another, &c.

Compound Pronouns

composed in English of, "ever, soever," are expressed by *go-rúng*, or *gang la*, thus, *to go-rúng*, or *to gang la*, whoever, whosoever; *sa-re go-rúng*, or *sa-re gang la*, whichever whichsoever, whatsoever; *shú go-rúng*, or *shú gang la*, whatever, whatsoever; *sa-tet go-rúng*, or *sa-tet gang la*, how much soever, &c.

All may be declined, as already shown.

9.—*Of Verbs.*

In Lepcha, the form of verbs is unaltered by Number or Gender of the governing Noun, and their roots (with one or two exceptions) remain unchanged by Tense.

The Conjugation, is like the Declension of Substantives, performed by Postpositive Particles, or by the aid of an Auxiliary verb, (*shóp tyól*).

The root of the verb may be taken for the Infinitive, thus, *shi*, to see; *lik*, to call; *mát*, to do, to which root the Particles indicative of tense may be affixed. These Particles are sometimes very indefinite. Some of them may, at times, be made to denote different tenses, or they may often altogether be dispensed with, the sense being shown by the context.

The following exemplification, however, may be taken as a guide for the formation of tenses.

The Indicative Mood.

Present Tense.

The Present Tense may be formed by affixing, to the root, the auxiliary verb *bám*, (literally to remain); also sometimes by, *ngán*, (literally to sit,) thus, *go lik bám*, I call, or am calling.

The Past

may be denoted by the Particle *bá*, as *lik bá*, called, or have called, but in general the simple root stands for the past, thus, *go lik yáng na hó ma thyo ne*, I called, but you did not hear me; *go ayo á-re li*, I said this before.

The Pluperfect

may be indicated by the addition of the word, *fát*, either, in combination with, or without the past particle *bá*, thus, *lik fát*, or *lik fát bá*, had called; *hó di wung sa na-hán hu zúk fát*, before you came, he had done it; (*fát*, is a verb itself, signifying to lose, to be lost, hence by an hyperphrasis, implying what is gone, past).

The Future

is expressed by the affixed particle, *sho*, thus, *lik sho*, I shall call.

The Future Perfect

may be rendered by a conjunction of the Past and Future terms; thus, *lik fát sho*, shall have called, *hó di wung sa na-hán go zúk fát sho*, before you return, I shall have finished it.

The Subjunctive Mood

expressing contingency is formed in the

Present Tense

by affixing, to the root of the verb, the particle ᰎᰫ *pú*, thus, ᰜᰧᰭ ᰎᰫ *lik pú*, may perhaps call.

The Imperfect.

This tense is indefinite. It may equally with the Future Indicative, be represented by the particle ᰡᰨ *sho*, and sometimes by the participle particle ᰡᰵ *shang*, or it may simply be understood by the context. Might, could, would, and should, imply permission, power, obligation, and desire, so may be expressed by verbs or words bearing these significations.

The Past Tense

may be formed by affixing the particle of contingency to the root of the verb, or to the past sign, thus, ᰜᰧᰭ ᰎᰫ *lik pú*, or ᰜᰧᰭ ᰒᰦᰳ ᰎᰫ *lik fát pú*, may, would, (might, &c.,) perhaps have called; ᰝᰩ ᰕ ᰍᰩᰲ ᰍ ᰃᰵ ᰃᰨ ᰣᰦᰊᰱ ᰓᰨ ᰎᰫ *hó ma nón na gang go á-dom bo pú*, if you had not gone, I might have given you it.

The Future

may be expressed by the particle ᰡᰵ *shang*, combined with the particle of contingency, thus, ᰜᰧᰭ ᰡᰵ ᰎᰫ *lik shang pú*, shall perhaps call.

The Imperative.

2nd Person. Singular and Plural

is rendered by the affixed particle ᰣᰨ *o*; or, should the verb end in a consonant, by the reduplication of the final consonant with, or without the addition of the particle ᰣᰨ *o*, thus, ᰜᰧ ᰣᰨ *lĩ o*, speak; ᰊᰧ ᰣᰨ *dĩ o*, come, (thou or ye); ᰜᰧᰭ ᰀ *lik ka*, or ᰜᰧᰭ ᰀ ᰣᰨ *lik ka o*, call; ᰕᰦᰳ ᰊ *mát ta*, or ᰕᰦᰳ ᰊ ᰣᰨ *mát ta o*, do, perform; ᰊᰵ ᰅ *dãng nga*, or ᰊᰵ ᰅ ᰣᰨ *dãng nga o*, run, (thou or ye). The particle ᰣ *a*, may, though rarely employed, be affixed to the verb terminating in a vowel, thus, *li a*, or *li a o*, speak thou (or ye).

With reference to the Persons in the Objective case, the Imperative is expressed by *kón*, and may be declined in the Persons; thus, *ka-sum*, *ka-nyum*, *hum*, *ka-yúm*, *hu-yúm lik kón*, let me, us two, him (her or it), us, them call.

The word *kón*, is a verb implying—to let, to permit,—the above form is therefore merely putting the verb, *lik*, in the Infinitive, and *kón*, in the 2nd Person Imperative, and so it will be apparent when written in full; thus, *hó nun hum lik kón na o*, let, or permit thou him to call.

When a verb, ending in a vowel, is succeeded by *kón*, the final is amplified by the euphonic consonant termination appertaining to it; thus,

nyi, to have, to possess.	*nyim, kón*, let him (her or it), possess.
shi, to see.	*shim kón*, let him, &c., see.
zú, to live.	*zúm kón*, let him, &c., live.
byi, to give.	*byin kón*, let him, &c., give.
li, to speak.	*lin kón*, let him, &c., speak.
di, to come.	*dít kón*, let him, &c., come.

But, as shown under the head of adjectives, all words do not admit of paragoge; in this case, such verbs would of course retain their final vowel; thus,

má, to be secret.	*má kón*, let it be secret.
dá, to lie.	*dá kón*, let him, &c., lie.
po, to flit, to migrate.	*po kón*, let him, &c., flit.

The 2nd Person Imperative is also sometimes expressed, by prefixing the particle *ta*, and affixing *ka*, or *sa*, to the verb; thus, or *hum ta mát sa*, or, *ta mát ka*, let him do it.

There is also a Particle *ká*, which, when succeeding a verb, gives a plural hortative or a postulate signification. It is evidently composed of the substantive verb *ka*, and the optative particle *á*. Verbs, ending in a vowel, when preceding it, are not inflected; thus, *li* (not *lin*) *ká*, let us speak.

Participles.

The Present (and Gerund)

is formed, if the verb ends in a vowel, by affixing the particle *ung*, or *wung*, or, if ending in a consonant, by reduplicating in the Participle sign, the final consonant; thus, *shi wung*, seeing; *li wung*, speaking; *mát tung*, doing; *rok kung*, reading; *dang, ngung*, running, &c.

The Past

is formed by affixing, to the root of the verb, the particle *bán;* thus, *lik bán*, having called; *hu zúk bán, nón*, having done it, he went.

bán, may be considered to be a synæreses of the particle *bá*, and the conjunction *un;* thus, *hu zúk bá, un nón*, he did it, and went. *bán*, is often abbreviated to *ban*.

The Future Indefinite (and Gerund)

is indicated by the particle *shang;* thus, *lik shang*, calling, about calling. (Gerund) *hó sa-re mát shang re khók bo nyi sho* thou shalt be responsible for all thy doings (deeds).

The Future Definite

is denoted by affixing, to the Present Participle sign, the particle *sa,* thus, *lik kung sa,* when, or on calling; and a

Future Exact

may be formed by affixing, to the above, the particle *la,* thus, *lik kung sa la,* immediately on calling.

The Future Perfect

may be expressed by the particle *shen,* thus, *lik shen,* when having called. *shen,* is, however, often used indefinitely.

The Conjunctive Participle

is formed by the particle *lung,* thus, *lik lung,* calling.

An Emphatic Participle

may be rendered by the particle, *det,* thus, *lik det,* calling or just about to call. To this particle, the signs of the Tenses may be affixed, thus, *lik det bám,* am calling, or just about calling; *lik det bá,* was calling, or just about to call; *lik det pú,* may perhaps be calling, &c.

Before *det,* verbs, ending in a vowel, assume their final consonant, thus, *lin det,* about speaking; *dit det,* coming, just about to come.

Passive Voice.

The passive voice is formed by the aid of an auxiliary verb; or more commonly expressed through the medium of the Instrumental case, thus, the sentence, *hu nun zúk,* may be rendered, he did it, or it was done by him.

The Active, or Passive signification of a verb, is generally sufficiently indicated by the sense of the context. But when it is requisite to make use of the passive voice, it may be formed by affixing to the verb, with a substantive verb combined, *thóm bo*, the adjective, or agentive form of *tho*, to place; or *nón*, the preterite of *nóng*, to go.

The former *thóm bo*, denotes a local relation, and represents the seat of the object or action, and when combined with a substantive verb, renders the active verb to which it is affixed, passive, thus, *pi̴*, to write, *pi̴ thóm bo*, written, *pi̴ thóm bo gum*, it is written; *nyet*, to show, *nyet thóm bo*, shown, *nyet thóm bo gum*, it is shown; *má*, to hide, *má thóm bo*, hidden, *má thóm bo gum*, it is hidden, &c.

The latter *nón*, implies an absolute transition, and infers directly, or inversely, the object to have gone, past,—or been, and may be affixed to all verbs to which that sense is desired to be conveyed; combined with a substantive verb, it forms a passive voice, thus, *mók*, to expend, *mók nón*, expended, to be expended, *mók nón gum*, is expended; *mák*, to die, *mák nón*, dead, to be dead, *mák nón gum*, is dead; *lók*, to injure, *lók nón gum*, is injured; *nyak*, to shake, *nyak nón gum*, is shaken.

The agentive *nón bo*, may be affixed instead of the simple preterite, *nón*, but this form is unnecessary.

Some verbs are, in themselves, Intransitive or Passive, thus, *kri̴*, to be bitter, *chor*, to be sour; *klyám*, to be sweet; *nyung*, to be deep; *sáp*, to be shallow, &c. These verbs may be conjugated similarly to the active voice of transitive verbs.

Some verbs may have both an Active and Passive signification, thus, *lók*, to injure, or be injured; *dak*, to hurt, to be hurt, to be sick; *go lók bám*, I am injuring, or am injured; *hum ma dak kun*, do not hurt him; ᰝᰪ ᰌᰭ ᰓᰦᰮ *hu dak bám*, he is ill, &c. The addition of the substantive verb, ᰃᰪᰮ *gum*, would, however, render the Passive voice of these verbs unmistakable, as, ᰃᰨ ᰜᰩᰭ ᰃᰪᰮ *go lók gum*, I am injured, &c.

To the above, as also to all Passive verbs, the affixing of ᰍᰩᰰ *nón*, imparts to the verb an acquisitive condition, thus, ᰝᰪ ᰌᰭ ᰍᰩᰰ *hu dak nón*, he has become ill; ᰝᰪ ᰀᰥᰧ ᰍᰩᰰ *hu kri nón*, it has become bitter.

ᰍᰩᰰ *nón*, when affixed to some active transitive verbs, occasionally retains its literal sense of "to go" thus, ᰜᰧᰭ ᰍᰩᰰ *lik nón*, though it may imply, "called," would be more commonly understood to signify, "gone to call," so, ᰝᰪ ᰜᰧᰭ ᰍᰩᰰ ᰃᰪᰮ *hu lik nón gum*, he has gone to call; but this is merely an elliptical form of ᰜᰧᰭ ᰡᰵ ᰀᰦ ᰍᰩᰰ *lik shang ká nón*, therefore in its entirety the sentence would be written, ᰝᰪ ᰍᰪᰰ ᰝᰪᰮ ᰜᰧᰭ ᰡᰵ ᰀᰦ ᰍᰩᰰ *hu nun hum lik shang ká nón*, he has gone for the purpose of calling him.

Verbal Particles.

There are numerous particles, affixed to verbs, which are for the most part of indefinite meaning, such are ᰕ *ma*, ᰕ ᰣᰨ *ma o*, ᰚᰮ ᰣᰨ *yam o*, ᰠ ᰣᰨ *sa o*, ᰎᰛᰩ *pa-ró*, ᰊᰫᰵ *túng*, &c.

The first three, generally, represent the Present or Past tenses, thus, ᰃᰨ ᰎᰧ ᰕ *go pi ma*, I am writing or have written; ᰝᰪ ᰋᰧ ᰕ ᰣᰨ *hu thi ma o*, he has arrived; ᰝᰪ ᰕᰦᰭ ᰚᰮ ᰣᰨ *hu mák yam o*, he is dead. ᰠ ᰣᰨ *sa o*, applies more to the present or future, thus, ᰃᰨ ᰍᰩᰵ ᰠ ᰣᰨ *go nóng sa o*, I shall go. ᰎᰛᰩ *pa-ró*, generally, implies a doubt, as ᰃᰨ ᰡᰧ ᰎᰛᰩ *go shi pa-ró*, I may possibly see him. ᰊᰫᰵ *túng* is used, especially, in the Imperfect Subjunctive, thus, ᰚᰨ ᰕ ᰃᰨ ᰍ ᰃᰵ ᰃᰨ ᰍᰪᰰ ᰣᰚᰫᰮ ᰜᰧ ᰊᰫᰵ *yo ma go na gang go nun á-yúm li túng*, if it were not so, I would have told you. But when, through the context, the meaning is evident, these particles are sometimes used, independent of tense, merely to give fulness and completion to the sentence. Rules, however, only require to be laid down to render these and such relative particles, definite and absolute.

pá, is a verbal affix, giving a slight degree of emphasis, thus, *ryú pá*, it is good; *um pá*, it is nice; (it corresponds to the Tibetan verbal termination པ *pa*).

ne, is a particle attached to *nón*, giving emphasis to the past, thus, *nón ne*, gone, *hu mák nón ne*, he has expired, *kó pla nón ne*, the order hath gone forth. (This *ne*, is identical with ནས *nas*, the Tibetan Pluperfect sign.)

dá, and *che na*, are Adverbial Particles, giving emphasis to the verb, whether the latter be expressed or understood, thus *á-lo dá*, it is certainly so; *go nóng che na*, I shall positively go.

Of Substantive Verbs.

The Substantive Verb, to be, may be expressed by *gum*, *gó*, *go*, *gá*, *ka*, and *nyi*, which all represent, am, art, is, are, were, &c. Each, however, in a degree bear separate applications, thus,

gum, is, generally, used relatively with all the Numbers and Persons, so, *go gum*, I am, *hu gum*, he is, *á-nyi gum*, you two are, *á-yú gum*, you are. It is also used interrogatively, where the subject, in the Objective case, is expressed, thus, *hó sa-re zang sa ma-ró gum*, what kind of person art thou?

gó, is more usually employed in the 2nd Person, and especially interrogatively, thus, *hó gó*, thou art; *hó to gó*, who art thou? *á-yú sa-bá nóng shang gó*, where art thou going? *hu shú mát tung gó*, what is he doing?

go, is used more relatively, and in negation, and without regard to person, thus, *go ma go ne*, it is not I; *go pá*, it is; *á-lo la ma go ne*, it is not even this. When unconnected with person, it is used interrogatively in preference to *gó;* thus, *á-lom shú mát go shang a*, why should it be so? *á-re shú go te*, what can this be?

gá, is almost wholly confined to the negative, thus, *ma gá ne*, it is not.

ka, is almost invariably combined with a particle, and generally refers relatively to a neuter subject, thus, *á-re shú ka te*, what may this be; *shú ka go-rúng*, whatever it may be, *ka che na*, it certainly is; *ka gang la*, even if it were.

gum, and *ka*, are seldom, if ever, used with the negative particles affixed.

Of Conjugation.

gum, and *gó*, am, art, is, are, were, represent the present and sometimes the past, they are not capable of being conjugated, not admitting of the Particles of conjugation being affixed to them.

ka, may have emphatic, and adverbial, particles affixed, but does not bear conjugation.

go, may be conjugated in the Active voice, it is chiefly used, irrelative of person, thus, *á-re go sho*, this shall be, this will do; *o-lom go bá*, it was so; *sa-lom go shang a*, how shall it be?

gá, may be conjugated similarly to *go*, but chiefly in the negative form, thus, *ma gá na sho*, it shall not be; *sa-thá la ma gá na bá*, it never was.

nyi, may be conjugated in all the tenses, and when affixed to other verbs, forms a past tense, and sometimes a passive voice, thus, *hu nyi bám*, he is; *hu bám nyi*, he was, he was present; *hu nun zúk nyi*, it was done by him.

The following are examples of verbs conjugated.

gum, am, art, &c.

Singular.	Dual.
go gum, I am.	*ka nyi gum*, we two are.
hó gum or *gó*, thou art.	*á-nyi gum*, you two are.
hu gum, he is.	*hu-nyi gum*, they two are.

Plural.

ka-yú gum, we are.

á-yú gum, or *gó*, ye are.

hu-yú gum, they are.

nyi, am, was, were, have, &c.

go nyi, I was.	*ka-nyi nyi*, we two were.
hó nyi, thou wast.	*á-nyi nyi*, you two were.
hu nyi, he was.	*hu-nyi nyi*, they two were.

Plural.

ka-yú nyi, we were.

á-yú nyi, ye were.

hu-yú nyi, they were.

nyi bám, am being.

nyi fát, was, have, has been, had been.

nyi fát bá, had, had been.

nyi fát sho, shall have been.

nyi pú, may be, may have, may have been.

nyi fát pú, may have been, had perhaps been.

nyi shang pú, may, might, would perhaps have been.

nyim kón, let me, us, be; let us have.

nyi o, be thou or ye; have thou or ye.

nyi ká, let we be; let we have.

nyi wung, being, having.

nyi bán, having, having been.

nyi shang, about being; about having.

nyi wung sa, when being, or when having.

nyi wung sa la, immediately on being, or having.

nyi lung, being, having.

nyim det, being, or just about being, or having.

As the root of the verb is uninflected by number or person, it will in the following paradigma, be sufficient to show the 1st person of each tense.

shak, to advise.

Active Voice.

Indicative Mood.

Present Tense.

go shak, I advise.

go shak bám, I am advising.

Past Tense.

go shak, I advised.

go shak bá, I advised, or was advising.

go shak fát, I have advised.

go shak fát bá, I had advised.

Future Tense.

go shak sho, I shall advise.

Future Perfect.

go shak fát sho, I shall have advised.

Subjunctive Mood.

Present Tense.

go shak pú, I may perhaps advise.

Imperfect, Past, and Future Perfect.

go shak sho,
go shak shang, } I may, might, would advise or have advised.

go shak pú,
go shak shang pú,
go shak fát pú, } I may, might, would perhaps advise, or may, might, &c. perhaps have advised.

Imperative Mood.

hó shak kón, advise thou.

á-nyi shak kón, advise you two.

á-yú shak kón, advise ye.

Hortative.

ka-nyi shak ká, let we (us) two advise.

ka-yú shak ká, let we (us) advise.

Participles.

Present and Gerund.

shak kung, advising.

Past.

shak bán, having advised.

Future, Indefinite and Gerund.

shak shang, advising, about advising.

Future, Definite.

shak kung sa, when or on advising.

Future Exact.

shak kung sa la, immediately on advising.

Future Perfect.

shak shen, when having advised.

Conjunctive.

shak lung, advising.

Emphatic.

shak det, advising, or just about advising.

Passive Voice.

The Passive voice, as already explained (in pages 49 and 50) may, when necessary, be conjugated by aid of the verb *nón*, or the Agentive *thóm bo*, and a substantive verb affixed, thus,

---

Indicative Mood.

Present Tense.

go shak nón gum,
go shak thóm bo gum, } I am advised.

Past Tense.

go shak nón bá,
go shak thóm bo nyi, } I was, or have been advised.
go shak thóm bo nyi bá,

Future Tense.

go shak nón sho, *go shak thóm bo n̄yi sho,*	I shall have been advised.

And so on, the Particles indicative of the tenses, may be affixed to the Passive signs.

Deponent Verbs.

May be conjugated, thus.

ryú, to be good.

Indicative Mood.

Present Tense.

go ryú bám, I am good.

Past Tense.

go ryú, *go ryú bá,* *go ryú n̄yi,* *go ryú n̄yi bá,*	I was, have been, had been good.

Future Tense.

go ryú sho, I shall be good.

Future Perfect Tense.

go ryú n̄yi sho, *go ryú sho bá,* *go ryú n̄yi sho bá,*	I shall have been good.

Subjunctive Mood.

Present Tense.

go ryú bám pú, I may perhaps be good.

Imperfect.

go ryú sho, } I might, would be good.
go ryú shang, }

go ryú shang pú, I might would perhaps be good.

Perfect.

go ryú pú, } I may have been good.
go ryú ñyi pú, }

Pluperfect.

go ryú ñyi bá pú, I had perhaps been good.

Future Perfect.

go ryú ñyi sho pú, I shall perhaps have been good.

Imperative Mood.

ka-sum ryúm kón, let me be good.
hó ryú o, be thou good.
hum ryúm kón, let him be good.
á-ñyi ryú o, be you two good, &c.
ka-yúm ryúm kón, let us be good.
a-yú ryú o, be ye good.
hu-yúm ryúm kón, let them be good.

Hortative.

ka-yú ryú ká, } let we (us) be good.
ká ryú ká, }

Participles.

Present.

ryú wung, being good.

Past and Conjunctive.

ryú bán, having been good.

Future Indefinite.

ryú shang, about being good.

Future Definite.

ryú wung sa, when, or on being good.

Future Exact.

ryú wung sa la, immediately on bein g good.

Future Perfect.

ryú shen, when having been good.

Conjunctive.

ryú lung, being good.

Emphatic.

ryúm det, being, or just about being good.

Irregular Verbs.

nóng, to go; *hróng*, to rise; and *fróng*, to point out, to indicate; inasmuch as they differ from other verbs, by bearing an inflected form in the Past Tenses; may be said to be irregular. They may be thus conjugated.

nóng, to go.

Active Voice.

Indicative Mood.

Present Tense.

go nóng bám, I am going.

Imperfect.

ᰃᰨ ᰍᰨᰵ ᰓᰦ *go nóng bá*, I was going.

Perfect.

ᰃᰨ ᰍᰨᰰ *go nón*, I went, I have gone.

Pluperfect.

ᰃᰨ ᰍᰨᰰ ᰓᰦ *go nón bá*, I had gone.

Future.

ᰃᰨ ᰍᰨᰵ ᰡᰨ *go nóng sho*, I shall go.

Future Perfect.

ᰃᰨ ᰍᰨᰵ ᰡᰨ ᰓᰦ *go nóng sho bá*, I shall have gone.

Subjunctive Mood.

Present Tense.

ᰃᰨ ᰍᰨᰵ ᰎᰪ *go nóng pú*, I may perhaps go.

Imperfect.

ᰃᰨ ᰍᰨᰵ ᰡᰨ *go nóng sho*, } I would go.
ᰃᰨ ᰍᰨᰵ ᰡᰵ *go nóng shang*, }

Perfect.

ᰃᰨ ᰍᰨᰰ ᰎᰪ *go nón pú*, I may perhaps have gone.

Future.

ᰃᰨ ᰍᰨᰵ ᰡᰵ ᰎᰪ *go nóng shang pú*, I would, or, perhaps shall go.

Future Perfect.

ᰃᰨ ᰍᰨᰰ ᰡᰵ ᰎᰪ *go nón shang pú*, I would, or, shall perhaps have gone.

Imperative.

ᰀᰠᰮ ᰍᰨᰰ ᰀᰨᰰ *ka-sum nón kón*, let me go.

ᰝᰨ ᰍᰨ ᰣᰨ *hó no o*, go thou.

ᰝᰮ ᰍᰨᰰ ᰀᰨᰰ *hum nón kón*, let him go.

ka-nyum nón kón, let us two go.

á-nyi no o, go you two.

hu-nyum nón kón, let them (those) two go.

ka-yúm nón kón, let us go.

á-yú no o, go ye.

hu-yúm nón kón, let them go.

Hortative.

ka-yú ná,
ká nóng ká, } let we (us) go.

Postulate.

ka-yú ná ya,
ka-yú ná le, } Let we (us) go, come along, do come along.

Participles.

Present (and Gerund).

nóng ngung, going.

Past.

nón bán, having gone.

Future Indefinite (and Gerund).

nóng shang, about going.

Future Definite.

nóng ngung sa, when, or, on going.

Future Exact.

nóng ngung sa la, immediately on going.

Future Perfect Tense.

nón shen, when having gone.

Conjunctive.

nóng lung, going.

Emphatic.

nón det, just about going.

Passive Voice.

As in English, Intransitive Verbs are not considered to bear a Passive Voice, so in Lepcha, the tenses of these verbs in the Indicative, and Subjunctive Moods, for instance, *go nón gúm*; *go nón nyi bá*; *go nón nyi sho*; &c., may be regarded as only the Preterite Tense, Indicative Mood, with an auxiliary verb conjugated and affixed. Moreover, "I am gone," "I have been gone," "I shall have been gone," &c., may, perhaps, be looked on as questionable orthology.

This form of speech, however, is in Lepcha seldom used, but the Imperative and some of the Participles are employed in the Passive, and being expressed without the aid of an Auxiliary verb, may be deemed to be a true conjugation, and in locution, to be logically correct, thus—

Imperative Mood.

nón na o, be thou (you two, or ye) gone.

Hortative.

nón ká, let we (us) be gone.

Postulate.

nón ka le, do let we (us) be gone.

Participles.

Present Tense.

nón nung, being gone.

Future Tense.

ᰍᰨᰰ ᰍᰪᰵ ᰝ *nón nung sa*, when, or, on being gone.

Future Exact.

ᰍᰨᰰ ᰍᰪᰵ ᰝ ᰜ *nón nung sa la*, immediately on being gone.

Conjunctive.

ᰍᰨᰰ ᰜᰪᰵ *nón lung*, being gone.

The Past Participles would necessitate the addition of an auxiliary verb, thus, ᰍᰨᰰ ᰆᰧ ᰓᰦᰰ *nón nyi bán*, having been gone. This form, as, has been already stated, would be seldom resorted to.

In like manner may be conjugated the verb, ᰠᰥᰨᰵ *hróng*, to rise, to ascend; Past, ᰠᰥᰨᰰ *hrón*, ascended; Imperative, ᰠᰥᰨ *hro*, ascend (thou, or, ye). Also, ᰑᰥᰨᰵ *fróng*, to point out, to indicate; Past, ᰑᰥᰨᰰ *frón*, indicated. ᰑᰥᰨᰵ *fróng*, has, however, no inflected form of Imperative, nor has, either of these two verbs, a separate form for the Hortative, corresponding to ᰍᰦ *ná*.

Neuter Verbs.

to be conjugated, require the aid of an Auxiliary verb, thus,

ᰊᰨᰯ *thól*, to be near.

Present Tense.

ᰃᰨ ᰊᰨᰯ ᰓᰦᰮ *go thól bám*,
ᰃᰨ ᰊᰨᰯ ᰆᰧ ᰓᰦᰮ *go thól nyi bám*, } I am near.

Past Tense.

ᰃᰨ ᰊᰨᰯ ᰆᰧ *go thól nyi*,
ᰃᰨ ᰊᰨᰯ ᰆᰧ ᰓᰦ *go thól nyi bá*, } I was, have been, or, had been near.

Future Tense.

ᰃᰨ ᰊᰩᰯ ᰐᰧ ᰡᰨ *go thól nyi sho,* I shall be near.

Future Perfect Tense.

ᰃᰨ ᰊᰩᰯ ᰐᰧ ᰓᰦᰳ ᰡᰨ *go thól nyi fát sho,* I shall have been near.

Subjunctive Mood.

ᰃᰨ ᰊᰩᰯ ᰐᰧ ᰎᰪ *go thól nyi pú,*
ᰃᰨ ᰊᰩᰯ ᰐᰧ ᰡᰵ ᰎᰪ *go thól nyi shang pú,* } I may, might, would, perhaps be, or, perhaps have been, near.

Imperative Mood.

ᰝᰩ ᰊᰩᰯ ᰐᰧ ᰣᰨ *hó thól nyi o,* be thou near.

ᰣᰦᰛᰪ ᰊᰩᰯ ᰐᰧ ᰣᰨ *á-yú thól nyi o,* be ye near.

Participles.

ᰊᰩᰯ ᰐᰧ ᰟᰪᰵ *thól nyi wung,* being near.

And so on, affixing the participle signs to, ᰐᰧ *nyi,* as shown in page 55.

Common Verbs

having both an Active and Passive signification, may have the Passive Voice rendered more definite by affixing to the root of the verb, an Auxiliary verb, thus, ᰜᰩᰭ *lók,* to injure or be injured ; ᰃᰨ ᰜᰩᰭ ᰒᰦᰮ *go lók bám,* I am injuring ; ᰃᰨ ᰜᰩᰭ ᰒᰦ *go lók bá,* I was injuring, or was injured ; ᰃᰨ ᰜᰩᰭ ᰡᰨ *go lók sho,* I shall injure, or shall be injured ; ᰃᰨ ᰜᰩᰭ ᰃᰪᰮ *go lók gum,* I am injured ; ᰃᰨ ᰜᰩᰭ ᰐᰧ *go lók nyi,* I am, was, or, have been injured ; ᰃᰨ ᰜᰩᰭ ᰐᰧ ᰒᰦ *go lók nyi bá,* I have been, or, had been injured, &c.

PART IV.

PARTS OF SPEECH.

Derivative, and Primitive.—Etymology.

Of Adverbs.

Adverbs may be formed, from verbs, by affixing to the root the Particle *la*, thus,

ryú, to be good.	*ryú la*, goodly, well.
jan, to be bad.	*jan la*, badly.
gyum, to be cautious.	*gyum la*, cautiously.
tóm, to be strong, to be firm.	*tóm la*, strongly, firmly.
zak, to be right.	*zak la*, rightly, correctly.
ryám, to be handsome.	*ryám la*, handsomely.
són, to be dry.	*són la*, dryly.
shel, to be wet.	*shel la*, wetly.
chóng, to be swift.	*chóng la*, swiftly.
jel, to have correct pronunciation.	*jel la*, pronouncing correctly.

Some Adverbs thus formed, may take a prefixed Particle or Syllable, thus—

ba, to be full.	*ba la*, *pa-ba la*,	full, brimful.
gal, to disappear.	*gal la*, *sa-gal la*,	disappearingly.

fli, to separate, to be separate.	*fli la*, *pur-fli la*,	separately.
gli, to be distinct.	*gli la*, *sa-gli la*,	distinctly, clearly.
nók, to be black.	*nók la*, *nuk-nók la*,	blackly.
náng, to be straight.	*náng la*, *nung-náng la*,	straightly.

The last two are examples of words that may be adverbially expressed by means of the Substantive or Adjective prefixed particle *á*; thus, *á-nók mát*, or, *nók la mát*, to make black, to blacken; *á-náng tho*, or, *náng la tho*, to place straight.

But many Adverbs, though thus formed, possess no verbal root, the following are examples:—

pur-shú la, untidy, slovenly.

tot la, *pur-tot la*, unpolished, roughly.

ta-dár la, curved outwards.

pa-grók la, slightly apart.

sa-rin la, convulsively, spasmodically.

rum-róm la, bulging out in centre, ventricose.

fuk-fyek la, worn by friction.

ra-rá la, standing on end, bristling up (as hair), &c.

sa-du la, slowly.

tum-tom la, swollen out.

Adverbs may also be formed by reduplication, or, by the addition of a chime word, with or without an epenthesis, thus,

song nga song nga, reverberating, resonantly.

thár ra thor ra, scattered about, here and there.

kár kár, / *kár ra kár ra*, — curling, twistingly.

hyak ka hyak ka, pointed, tapering to a point.

kryóm kryóm, unitedly, concordantly.

hyam ma hyam, quietly, smoothly, gently and noiselessly.

shil la shól la, confusedly, higgledy-piggledy, hurley-burley.

Adverbs may likewise be sometimes expressed by the reduplication of a substantive, thus, *sa-ayák*, a day, *sa-ayák sa-ayák*, daily; *nám*, a year, *nám nám*, yearly; *tók*, a drop, *tók tók*, drop by drop, guttatim.

Sometimes verbs in the Participle form may be made to qualify other verbs; hence performing the duty of Adverbs, thus—

ngak, to look, to observe, *ngak lung lóm*, to walk circumspectly; *kryóm*, to agree, to accord with, *kryóm lung zúk*, to act in concert, unanimously; *ching*, to think, to consider, *ching lung li*, to speak with reflection; *gó*, to rejoice, to be glad, *gó lung mát*, to do joyfully, gladly; *ngón*, to grudge, *ngón lung byi*, to give begrudgingly; *ro*, to fear, *ro lung nóng*, to go in fear, tremblingly.

A Substantive with a postposition, may also qualify the verb, thus—

á-yút ká bám, to live in sloth, sluggishly.

khor-de nun zúk, to act with prudence, prudently.

sák-ryút nun tyuk, to jump through joy, joyously.

á-thang nun li, to speak with truth, truly, truthfully.

sán-lat nun tsók, to bear with patience, patiently.

á-nyen sa dun byi, to inform with gentleness, gently.

The particle *la*, affixed to an adverb, gives intensity, thus—

sa-thá, when, *sa-thá la*, always, ever.

sa-bá, where, *sa-bá la*, everywhere.

chá, *á-nye*, *á-lang*, &c., are examples of Primitive Adverbs, having no verbal root, and no adverbial particle affixed. The following is a list of Adverbs, Primitive and Formative.

Adverbs of Time.

sa-thá, when. *sa-thá go-rúng*, whenever, whensoever.

sa-thá la, always, ever.

chá, just, just past. *chá á-lang*, just now (past).

á-lang, now. *á-lang do*, even now, this moment.

á-nye, presently. *tak la*, immediately.

fú la, shortly, in a few days. *ren*, since.

hán, before, first. *na-hán*, before, previously.

ayo, before, some time ago. *ayá*, before, formerly, a long time ago.

ayan-na ayan-na, long long ago, in former times, anciently.

á-lon, after, afterwards. *á-za ká*, in future.

á-lo bá, these times, now a days.

a'r nun pyil la, henceforth, henceforward.

sa-tshóng, when.

phyá, } in a short time, ere long, presently.
phyá la, }

á-tam á-tam, occasionally.

go-go, / *go-bá*, } sometimes.

á-tang, often.

bál bál, / *bál la bál la*, } by turns, over and over again, repeatedly.

na la, / *shúk-na*, / *shúk-na la*, } always, ever.

sa-thá la ma nyin ne, never.

tet, till, until. *ngól*, early, betimes.

blin la, late, behind hand, too late. *phi la*, late, too late.

The following may be considered more as nouns expressed, adverbially by reduplication, or, by the addition, of another adverb, or, of an adjective or post-position.

á-thyin á-thyin, at times, time by time.

kát-thyin, once, once on a time, some time.

kát-thyin kát-thyin, sometimes.

kám-thyin, seldom. *gróp-thyin*, frequently.

gyáp-thyin, many times, oft times.

kám-pát ká, in a short time, shortly, for a short time.

kám-pát ren, a short time since, lately.

á-pho á-pho, / *pho pho*, } at times, sometimes.

pho rel la, each time.

á-pho sa á-pho, time by time.

yut tet, for a moment, momentarily.

chhú-tshat chhú-tshat, hourly, horaly.

sa-ayák sa-ayák, daily, diurnally.

dun-hrók dun-hrók, weekly, hebdomadally.

la-vo la-vo, monthly.

nám nám, yearly. *nám kor ká*, by cycles of years.

nám gyó ká, by centuries.

ta-ayan, last year. *sum-byat*, next year.

sa-nyi ká, } by day. *so-náp ká*, by night.
sa-nyum ká, }

so-náp so-náp, nightly.

nap-mo ká, in the evening. *so-sóng ká*, at dawn.

sa-róng, to day. *sa-róng thok*, now-a-days.

lúk, } to-morrow. *lúk ká*, on the morrow.
lúk-kal, }

kát-tshóng ká, the day after to-morrow.

kát-chhám, three days hence. *kát-chhót*, four days hence.

ta-só, yesterday. *ayo-tshóng*, the day before yesterday.

ayo-chhám, three days ago. *ayo-chhót*, four days ago.

Adverbs of Place.

sa-bá, where.

sa-bi, where, (nearer and more definite than, *sa-bá*).

sa-bá go-rúng, wherever, wheresoever.

sa-bá la, everywhere. *sa-bá nun*, whence.

á-bá, here. *á-bi*, here, just here.

o-bá, there. *o-bi*, there, just there.

á-bá nun, hence. *á-bá ká*, hither.

o-bá nun, thence. *o-bá ká*, thither.

á-fi, here, (near) in this direction. *o-fi*, there (near), in that direction. *kát-fi*, somewhere, in some direction.

sa-lem, whether, in what way, in what direction.

a-lem, hither, in this way. *o-lem*, thither, in that way.

sa-bón, on what side. *á-bón*, on this side. *o-bón*, on that side.

á-pyin, on the other side, beyond.

a-tháng, above, up, here. *o-tháng*, above, up there.

á-thú, above, up above here. *o-thú*, above, up above there.

á-chhú, below, down here. *o-chhú*, below, down there.

sa-lo la, whither, which way.

á-lo la, hither, this way. *o-lo la*, thither, that way.

pe, *pe-a*, *pe-e*, *pe-bá*, *pe-fi*, *pe-lo la*, *pe-lol la*, *pe-lól la*, *pe-lon*, *pe-lon kón*, *pe-pe*, there, thither, that way, there in that direction, &c.

pi, *pi-bá*, there, thither. *pyar*, there, just there.

pyil,
pyil la, } there, thither, yonder.

pyil-ván, there, yonder, in that direction.

pyáp-pa, there, away yonder.

me, *me-a*, *me-ba*, *me-bi*, *me-lo la*, *me-lolla*, *me-lon*, down there, below yonder, there below (distant).

myil,
myil la, } below, down, under.

myil-ván,
myil kón, } downwards.

myil la myil la, down, far far down below.

tá, *tá-a*, *tá-á*, *tá-bá*, *tá-tháng*, above there, up there.

tál la, up above. *tál-ván*, upwards, aloft, on high.

to, *to-o*, *to-bá*, up there up, above (high).

to-thú, up above, over above. *to-lon*, upwards, straight upwards.

tul, *tul la*, up above, (high or far).

tul la tul la, above, high (or far away) above.

tul-ván, *tul-kón*, upwards, upward direction.

cho, *cho-o*, *cho-bá*, down there.

cho-chú, *cho-chhú*, *cho-chhú la* *cho-chhúl la*, down there below, low down, far below.

á-thól, near. *thól-bá*, near, nigh unto, at hand.

ma-rum, far. *ma-rum ma-rum*, far far, far away.

gyóm ká, to the right. *vim ká*, to the left.

The following are Postpositions as well as Adverbs.

á-plang, above, on, upon. *á-min*, below, under, underneath.

á-tón, above, over above, over-head. *tuk-dám*, above, over against.

sa-grám, below, beneath, underneath.

sa-gang, within, inside. *lyáng*, out, outside, &c.

Adverbs of Quality and Manner.

sa-lo, *sa-lom*, how, in what manner.

á-lom, this way, this manner, thus, so. *o-lom*, that manner, that way.

sa-lo la, *sa-lol la*, any way, any manner, every way.

sa-lo go-rúng, } any way whatsoever.
sa-lo gang la, }

náng la, evenly, straightly. 2 uprightly, straightforwardly, fairly, honestly.

gi la, divergingly, obliquely. 2 dishonestly, basely.

ling la, slopingly, inclinedly. 2 favouringly, partially, unfairly.

bát la, across, athwart. *fyók la*, transversely, intersectingly.

dyar-ra, parallel with, along side of. *pra la*, abreast.

dóp la, } opposite, vis-a-vis.
tyar la, }

tuk-fyón la, horizontally.

dyung la, vertically.

sa-bru la, obliquely, sideways. *klá la*, straightway, directly.

thung-kón, length-wise. *pyóng-kón*, breadth-wise.

ka-kyok la, crookedly, winding. *suk-jak la*, taperingly.

thán-na thyan-na, unevenly, irregularly. *plóng la*, evenly.

tóm la, strongly, stoutly. *hlu la*, weakly, feebly.

shik la, tightly. *hrung-hryong la*, loosely.

nur-ra nur-ra, gently, mildly, calmly.

nyen la, gently, meekly, good-naturedly. *sa-gang la*, gently, smoothly, softly, slowly. *num-ma num-ma*, softly, velvety.

yel la yel la, soft, sleeky, silky. *pur-nát la*, knotty, rugged.

yeng-nga yeng-nga, leisurely. *hlat la*, deliberately.

nyól nyól, slowly, lazily, sluggishly. *sa-du la*, slowly, gently.

sa-kyám la, gently, quietly, silently, tacitly.

gram, } quickly,
gram gram, } speedily.

hat-ta hat-ta, } hastily, passionately.
pa-kret la, }

kán la, excitedly, nervously. *fram la*, anxiously, apprehensively.

pa-brút la, roughly, ruggedly. *gryón-na*, harshly, gratingly.

zán-na, harshly, oppressively. *chom la*, oppressively, tyrannically.

dok la, conformably. *lyak la*, contrary to, reversely.

sa-kár la, suddenly, abruptly. *pó la*, becomingly, befittingly.

sa-lyon la, suddenly, unexpectedly, startingly.

sák-ta-lo la, unconsciously, absently. 2 by chance, accidentally.

jóm la, easily, with facility. *jo-di la*, conveniently, opportunely.

duk nun, *ka-tuk nun*, with difficulty, laboriously, troublesomely. *tyap la*, with difficulty, embarrassingly.

gyók la, bewilderingly, perplexingly. *go-thom la*, doubtfully, [dubiously.

sól la mól la, fickly, changeably, shilly-shally.

jem la, neatly, tidily. *mun-jú sa*, awkwardly, clumsily.

myong la, skilfully, masterly. *myá la*, diligently, devotedly.

jóng la, by practice, through experience. *fyóng-nga*, superficially.

kher la, skilfully, dextrously, adroitly, expertly, aptly.

sa-chen la, spontaneously. *prang la*, simultaneously.

dom la, concordantly, unanimously. *kóp la*, unitedly.

ma-ró do, naturally, of one's self.

ta-do bót tun, of one's own will, through one's own accord.

ti, *ti la*, } only, simply, merely, gratuitously. *pá-ta*, vainly, fruitlessly, uselessly, profitlessly.

ting-jók, at length, at last. *á-tyók ká*, in conclusion, finally.

Adverbs of Degree.

kám, a little. *kám zón*, only a little. *chup kám zón*, only a very little. *ik*, more, yet. *ik dá*, more again, yet more.

ik dá ik, more and more, again and again.

pur-tset. *pur-tshet*, partially, moderately.

rón la, middling, moderately. *dyóm la*, comparatively.

tĩ la, greatly, largely. *chu la*, smally, minutely.

chá, *chá chá*, *wong*, *wong wong*, enough, sufficient, plenty, stop, that will do, hold hand. *á-hlók*, more, over, above.

thák la, *khyóp la*, *jót la*, sufficiently, satisfyingly, amply, adequately, plentifully. *kãm la*, additively, supplementarily.

pa-pó la, proportionately. *pum-bróm la*, disproportionately.

thyil la, *á-thyil á-thyil*, successively, consecutively.

re re, *rel la*, each, respectively, specifically.

shãt-ta shãt-ta, one by one, drop by drop.

mán la, *báng la*, less, decreasingly, abatingly, attenuatingly.

pyón la, decreasingly, collapsingly, defectively.

bãt la, increasingly, augmentingly, developingly. *chóp la*, in addition, over, above, in excess. *vóng la*, abundantly, plentifully, profusely.

hlók la hlók la, *ling la*, superabundantly, redundantly.

nãm, *nãm-ma*, *nãm nãm*, *nyák-ka*, much, very, very much, exceedingly, excessively, extremely. *no-met*, too much.

pa-chák, almost, nearly. *kryol la*, almost, nearly all, about.

á-lúm, more, mostly, chiefly, principally, especially.

thyep-pa thyep-pa, perfectly, effectually, consummately, thoroughly.

phak-ka, *phin-dák-ka*, *pyal la*, altogether, completely, entirely, absolutely, utterly, downright, outright.

om-ma, wholly, entirely, completely, integrally, bodily, *en masse.*

gun-na, all, every, whole, entirely. *gun-jám la*, *sum-jám la*, all, wholly, totally. *tyang-nga*, altogether, entirely, completely.

thók la, perfectly, the utmost, culminatingly, to an acme, to a climax.

pál la, completely, perfectly, completively, finally.

Adverbs of Interrogation,

as, has already been shown, are expressed by *shú*, what? *sa-lom*, how? *sa-bá*, where? *sa-lem*, *sa-lon*, whither? *sa-thá*, when?

And compound, by, *shú-mát*, why, wherefore? *sa-lo gó*, how is it? *sa-re zang gó*, in what way? *shú tun-dók nun*, *shú kón nun*, for what reason, for what purpose, for what cause? &c.

Adverbs of Affirmation and Allegation

are chiefly formative, thus, *ak*, yes, ay, yea. *ak ma*, *ak ka che na*, yes, it is so, it certainly is so, &c.

á-lo go, *lo go*, *nyi ma-o*, it is so, be it so, so be it, &c.

go pá, (or *go pó*), *ayem bá*, (or *ayum bá*), certainly, truly, it is so, it is certainly, &c. *lo*, certainly, surely, undoubtedly.

thók chhat la, *tsó chhat la*, certainly, surely, assuredly, positively, indubitably. *un*, exactly, precisely, what else.

á-thang, *thang-nga*, *á-thang á-yáng*, *ngá la*, truly, verily, really, indeed, actually, in fact, in good truth.

The Negative Adverb

No, is expressed by *má-ne*, *mán*, or *mán-ne*. Other forms of negation will be hereafter given.

The qualifying term may be often expressed in the verb, thus—

phyá, to break asunder, to tear apart. *dyór*, to lean *against*.
dyón, to swell *out*. *vat*, to meet *round*, to *circum*vent. *ngól*, to put *aside*, to put *out of the way*. *tór*, to ward *off*, to guard *against*. *tek*, to knock *against*, to stumble *against*. *tshó*, to take *correct* aim, to shoot *well*.
phót, to burst *out*. *pla*, to issue *forth*.
chen, to cut *open*, to *dis*sect. *thót*, to separate *from*, to *de*tach.
chom, to be drawn *together*, to be *com*pressed. *tsu*, to meet *together*, to *con*join.
klá, to cut *through with one stroke*. *teng*, to cut *smoothly*, *evenly*.
thyak, to spring *upwards*. *klyót*, to leap *over*. *thet*, to jump *down*, *&c.*, *&c.*

2.—*Of Postpositions.*

The Part of Speech, which in European languages is generally represented by Prepositions, is in Lepcha chiefly expressed by Postpositive particles or words. These may be simple or compound, may be formed by the aid of adverbs, substantives, or verbs, or may be unexpressed, the tense being inherent in the verb.

Under the head of the Declension of nouns, some of the simple Postpositions have already been shown. But *sa*, *ká*, *nun*, besides bearing various applications, possess in their quality of Postpositions, other significations than merely those indicating the cases of nouns, for instance—

sa, of, implies also—for, with, along with, in, belonging to, regarding, concerning, with respect to, &c, thus.,—

pa-no sa pho-róng, the palace *of* the king.

thang shang sa sher, a glass *for* drinking out of.

zo zo sa ma nyin ne, there is no food *for* eating.

bán sa ngot, to cut *with* a knife.

shú sa pár sho, *with* what shall I buy it ?

hu sa nóng sho, I shall go *with* (*along with*) him.

go hó sa ma bám na sho, I shall not live *with* you.

hu sa á-gyáp nyi, he has much *belonging* (*appertaining*) *to* him.

la-yo sa ma bám mun, live not *in* (*in connection with*, or, *in performance of*) sin.

bu sa á-gyit, a generation *of* (*related to*) vipers.

á-yú khók sa hu gun-na thyo sho, he will listen to all *respecting* (or *concerning*) your affairs.

o-re sa sa-re go á-dom li re, *with reference to* (*with regard to*) that which I spoke to you of.

kóm gyó fa-ngo sa on, a horse *worth* (*worthy of*) five hundred rupees.

ká, to, also,—on, upon, over, in, at, for, for the purpose of, in case of, in the event of, in order that, &c., thus,—

hu ting ká nón, he has gone *to* the plains.

shing-te ká tho, place it *upon* the table.

tung-króm ká dyá, lay it *on* the floor.

á-kup ká dum ráng tho, spread the cloth *over* the child.

róm ká tháp, put it *in* (or, *into)* the box.

hu á-zóm á-than á-gyáp ká bám, he lives *in* (or, *in the midst of)* plenty.

shú ká, *for* what? for what purpose?

zo pár ká nón, gone *to* buy (*for the purpose of* buying) rice.

mak ká pók lung óp, take aim and fire *at* the target.

o-re to-tshat ká, *at* that time.

á-re sa-ayák ká, *on* this day.

hu ma di nung ká hó nóng khu, *in case of* (or, *in the event of)* his not coming you can go.

zú ká zóm gát, *to (in order to)* live, you must eat.

nun, from, by, also,—with, out, out of, and *sometimes*, through, on account of.

pat nun gyá-nók ká, *from* Tibet to China.

lyáng nun po, to depart *from* the place.

thám-bu nun á-re thá, this is eaten *by* insects.

hó ka-su nun thop, you obtained it *from* me.

mi nun ák, pluck it *out of* the fire.

go á-re nun dak bám, *through* (*on account of*, *owing to*) this, I am sick.

These Particles, though capable of giving expression to the above extended significations, are by no means the sole mode whereby such terms may be expressed. As Particles of Declension, however, they necessarily form an important part of speech, and are generally brought into conjunction with other words forming compound Postpositions.

The following are some examples of Postpositions (with applications).

á-plang, on, upon. *hláng-kó á-plang*, upon the shelf.

á-plang ká, on, over, above, moreover, besides. [gave clothes

á-zóm á-plang ká hu dum byi, besides food, he

ring gó á-dóm li re sa á-plang ká, over and above, the words which I spoke to you.

á-tón, over, above. *lá-ong á-tón hyan tho*, hang it over the lamp. *á-thyák á-tón*, above the head, over-head.

tuk-dám, above, over against. *jong re jang á-plang ká li kyong sa tuk-dám ding nyi*, the fortress stood on a hill, over against the town.

á-min, under, underneath. *gyá-ḥri á-min*, below the chair.

chho á-min, underneath the book.

sa-grám, below, under. *fat sa-grám*, below the ground.

hlo sa sa-grám úng-da dá nyi, a lake lay *at the base of* the hill.

na-hán, before. *á-lon*, after. *á-re á-tyan sa na-hán*, before this event. *so-sóng á-lon*, after day-break.

á-zut, *zut*, beside. *mi zut ngán-na*, sit beside the fire.

dyap, along with. *hu dyap no o*, go along with him.

tet, to, till, until. *á-yak nun á-tel tet*, from top to bottom.

mák tet go a-do sa nyi, till death I am yours.

fak la, throughout. *sa-nyi fak la*, throughout the day.

á-gún, without, void of. *á-zóm sa dum á-gún*, without food or clothes.

[Lepcha] *mán*, [Lepcha] *mán-pó*, [Lepcha] *mát*, except, besides, save. [Lepcha] *rum mán-pó á-ryúm zúk bo to la ma nyin ne*, except God, there is no one that doeth good. [I have nothing.

[Lepcha] *go dum-klok mát shú la ma nyin ne*, except a rag

[Lepcha] *á-bón*, on this side, cis. [Lepcha] *úng-kyong á-bón, on this side of* the river.

[Lepcha] *á-pyin*, on the other side, beyond, trans. [Lepcha] *gyám-tsho á-pyin*, beyond the ocean.

[Lepcha] *pa-hlyók*, astride. [Lepcha] *on pa-hlyók*, astride the horse.

[Lepcha] *prát la*, across. [Lepcha] *kúng lóm prát la dá*, the tree lay across the road. [Lepcha] *vyeng prát la bról*, bar it across the door.

[Lepcha] *sa-gang*, within, inside, amongst, amidst. [Lepcha] *á-fok sa-gang nun*, from amidst the debris. [Lepcha] *li sa-gang*, inside the house.

[Lepcha] *lyáng*, out, outside. [Lepcha] *tuk-pól lyáng tsak*, erect it outside the fence.

[Lepcha] *á-byek*, between, betwixt. [Lepcha] *phu-bo á-byek*, between the rails.

[Lepcha] *fi*, towards, in the direction of. [Lepcha] *nyót fi ká*, in the direction of the (cultivated) fields. [Lepcha] *pa-lik fi*, towards the open grounds.

[Lepcha] *kón*, towards, in the direction of, for, on account of, regarding, respecting, with reference to, &c. [Lepcha] *ná yá ḥrom kón lóm di le*, come let us walk towards the market. [Lepcha] *á-yú kón go á-re mát bám*, for you I am doing this. [Lepcha] *go nun á-yúm, hu mik-kráp bám yang li bá go hu sa mák kón li*, when I said to you that he sleepeth, I spoke with regard to his death. [Lepcha] *la-yo kón shú gom-thom la ma nyin ne sa-re gyú ká sa-thá la ma mát tun, with reference to* sin there can be no doubt *under* (*ká*,) any circumstances never commit it.

The above examples are likewise adverbs, and may be directly conjoined, or—with the exception of such as have the adverbial Particles affixed, (as, *fak la)*, or are affixes in themselves, (as, *fi)*—may be connected to the noun by a relative Particle, thus, *pun-hróp á-plang tho*, or, *sa á-plang tho*, place it on the mantel-piece. or, *li tuk-dám*, or, *sa tuk-dám*, over against the house, &c.

á-zut, is an adverb, adjective, or postposition, and literally means, close, near to, so, *mi á-zut*, *mi sa á-zut*, *mi zut ká*,—all imply—beside, close to, nigh to the fire.

The following are examples of Postpositions formed from nouns :—

lam ká, (from *á-lam*, a substitute) in room of, in place of, instead of.

á-re lam ká o-re bo, instead of this, give me that.

kur-vóng ká, (*kur-vóng*, front, presence), before, in front of.

hlá-góng kur-vóng ká, in front of the temple.

dun ká, (honorary presence), before, in presence of.

go pa-no dun ká nóng bám, I am going before (into the presence of) the king.

ta-gúm ká, (*ta-gúm*, the back), behind, at the back of, in the rear of.

gam-bo ta-gúm ká, behind the monastery.

nóng ká, (*nóng*, the interior), inside, within, among, amongst, amidst.

á-flik á-yú nóng ká, some among you. *á-re jók pro nóng ká*, in the midst of this tumult.

ka nun, (from *á-ka*, the hand), through, by means of.

go hu sa ka nun thop, I obtained it by means of him (through his patronage, power, authority).

lóm nun, (*lóm*, a road), through, by means of. *pi bo sa lóm nun khá-chhet thik sho*, the contract will be executed, through the medium of an agent. *bun lóm ma nyin ne*, there is no mode (way) of carrying it.

lyáng, (a place), of, the object of, the means of. *ngán lyáng*, a place for sitting, a sitting place. *thám-chang gun-na ká num-shim-nyo á-fyum lyáng gum*, to all animals, man is an object of awe.

ren, since. *á-dom shi ren to-tshat á-gyáp gúr nón ne*, since I saw you a long time has elapsed.

This word is evidently a synizesis of the article, *re*, and the postposition, *nun*; so, the above sentence may be written; 'from the time I saw you.' &c. It is also a Conjunction (see page 87).

Also the Postposition may be affixed to the verb, thus— *thór*, to be free; *thór lyáng ma nyin ne*, there is no means (way) of escaping.

The verb *mát*, is productive of numerous compound terms, thus—

mát bá, *nun mát bá*, *sa mát bá*, *mát bán*, *m t ren*, through, by means of, by reason of, &c., (literally, through being done). *ka-su nun mát bá*, through me. *sa-pó sa mát bá hu úng-kyong hyók*, by means of a raft he crossed the river. (or,) *ta-she do nun mát bán*, (or, *mát ren*), through, by means of Tashe himself.

The following are a few examples of postpositional terms, conveyed in the sense of the verb. [to *transfer*.

chĩm, to pour *over* anything. *dál*, to pour *from* one vessel *into* another.

tót, to hold *between* the teeth. *tóng*, to be covered *with* dirt.

sel, to stick *into*, to *insert*. *ryem*, to exult *over*, to triumph *over* another.

3.—*Of Conjunctions.*

Conjunctions are expressed simply or compositively. They may be primitives, or verbal formatives, or they may be rendered by Adverbs or Postpositions, and may be Co-ordinatives or Subordinatives, according to the relation they bear in the sentence.

The Copulative Conjunction,—and—is expressed by the Particle *sa*, thus, *hó sa go chhó nóng sho*, you *and* I will go together. *tyáng-mo sa sa-lók thám-chang á-tĩm sa shet nyĩm bo gum*, the elephant *and* rhinoceros are great *and* strong animals.

The Conjunctive Particle is often repeated after the connected word, this may have been affixed to effect a distinction between *sa*, the Postposition, and *sa*, the Conjunction; the two conjunctively also represent the co-relatives, both—and,—thus, *hó sa go ya*, might be understood to mean— I know you (about concerning you)—but the repetition of the *sa*, removes all ambiguity, so, *hó sa go sa ya*, you and I *both* know; hence, the above examples may be written, *tyáng-mo sa sa-lók sa thám-chang á-tĩm sa shet nyĩm bo gum*, *both* the elephant, *and* rhinoceros are animals great and strong; or, *tyáng-mo sa sa-lók thám-chang á-tĩm sa shet nyĩm bo sa gum*, the elephant and rhinoceros are animals, *both* great *and* strong.

un, is a co-ordinative conjunction chiefly connecting clauses and sentences. It bears also an additive sense and implies, yet, still, &c., thus— *óng thók nón un to-tshat glyáng ká yan-tan sa phyuk bo ngún nón*, the child grew up, *and* in the course of time, became learned and wealthy; *un á-re pang sa·á-lon*, *and* after these things; *un bo*, *yet*, *still* give (give more).

The Comparative Conjunction, *len*, than,—has already been explained under head of Degrees of Comparison (page 32).

The Conditional Conjunction, if, provided—is expressed by the verbal Particle *gang*, thus— *hó ching gang sák nón sho*, *if* you think, you will remember.

Its Correlative,—also, likewise—is represented by the emphatic Particle *la*, or, by the word, *gun*, thus, (or,) *hó mák gang go la*, (or, *go gun*,) *mák sho*, *if* you die, I shall die *also*.

The Disjunctive Conjunction,—except, unless,—is expressed also by *gang*, with the verb in the negative, thus, *á-yú fur la shir la ma pyet na gang ayok ke-chhi sa-re la thyep ma khun ne*, unless you diligently and perseveringly strive, you cannot accomplish any great work.

ren, since, as. *hó ta ya ren á-dom dun bo shong shú gát tung ma nyin ne*, since you know already (or, *from the* fact or circumstance of your knowing, &c., see page 84), there is no necessity to tell you.

gang la, *go-rúng*, are expressive Conjunctions, they imply—though, although, but, however, yet, albeit, nevertheless, notwithstanding, &c. They at the same time include their co-relative terms, thus— (or,) *ka-sum sót go-rúng*, (or, *gang la*,) *go ma mát na sho*, *although*, *even if* you kill me, *yet* I shall not do it.

yang, *yo*, thus, so.

The latter Conjunction, *yo*, and the verb *mát*, to do, in connection with *gang*, *gang la*, &c., form a number of compound conjunctive terms, thus—

yo gang, if so, in that case, then, &c.

yo gang la, although, be it so, nevertheless, &c.

yo ma go na gang, if it were not so, else, elsewise, otherwise.

yo bán, it being so, this being the case, &c.

yo ren, since it is so, in that case, &c.

a᷉r nun mát bá. *a᷉r nun mát bán*. *a᷉r nun mát lung*. *a᷉r mát ká*, on this account, hence, then, therefore, &c.

sa mát ren, since, hence, inasmuch as, forasmuch as.

The following are also Simple and Compound Conjunctions.

yáng la, but, still yet, however, nevertheless, notwithstanding.

yáng-na, either, or. *yáng-na á-re yáng-na o-re lya*, take either this or that.

shen la, is a significant conjunction, implying—then, but, yet, still, however, moreover, &c.

gán, is a simple and an expressive conjunction, signifying,—then, after that, thereupon, if so, in that case, since, therefore, &c.

a᷉r ren, since then, in that case, &c.

a᷉r plang ká, *a᷉r lyáng ká*, on this, thereupon, consequently, &c.

a᷉r kón ká, for this reason, on this account, hence, therefore.

dok la, *sa dok la*, *zang*, as, so, thus, accordingly, in like manner.

á-yú pát dok la ayek sho, as you sow, so shall you reap.

á-yú mát zang thop sho, according as you act, so shall you receive, &c.

The Compound Conjunction—for, in order that, for the purpose of, as already stated under the head of Postpositions, may be expressed by affixing the Particle *ká*, to the root of the verb; or it is more fully represented by combining the Postposition to the Future Participle, thus, *ma-ró sa chit tsak shang ká lyáng nóng*, to go out for the purpose of inquiring after a person's health. It may also be rendered by the nominal postposition *tun-dók ká*, for the purpose of, for the sake of, on account of—so, *hu sa lóm pa-náp mát tun-dók ká hum hryim mát*, to punish him, for the purpose of improving his ways. It may likewise be expressed by the verbal Particle *ta sa yang*, the first word preceding the verb, the two latter words succeeding, thus, *ma-ró ta pár sa yang thám á-ryám zúk*, to ornate an article, in order to induce a person to buy it, *num-shim-nyo ta tat sa yang jum-bo tóng*, to give alms, in order to obtain praise of man.

The adverbial Ordinals may be considered to be numerical conjunctions. These may be expressed by affixing to the cardinal numbers the Agentive Particle *bó*, or any one of the following nominal suffixes, *lyáng*, *kón*, *lóm*, combined with the postposition *ká*, thus, *kát bo ká*, in the first place, firstly, *nyat bo ká*, *nyat lyáng ká*, *nyat kón ká*, *nyat lóm ká*, in the second place, secondly. This form may be also rendered simply, by aid of the Postposition *sa*, expressed as a conjunction, thus, *kát sa*, with reference to the first, firstly, &c. *ting-jók ká*, *á-tyók ká*, at length, at last, may be also considered to be Adverbial Conjunctions.

Conjunction may be effected by means of the Conjunctive Participles, present, past or future; thus, *hu nóng lung zúk lel*, he finished it, as he went along, (literally, he going, along finished it); *hu nón bán zúk*, he went and did it, (literally, having gone, he did it); *hu-do li ká thi wung sa hu á-zóm zo sho*, on arriving at his home, he will eat his food; *shi wung sa la hu klo lung mák*, immediately on seeing it, he fell down dead, (fell down and died, or literally, falling, died).

The Particles of Declension may be combined with the Participles in forming Conjunction, thus, *hu-do sa á-bo sa mák re thyo wung ká, hu pya la nón*, on hearing of the death of his father, he fainted; (" *nun*," might here also be put in room of *ká*, to imply, 'through hearing, &c.' but it would generally be expressed in full, *nun mát bá*, &c.)*

The sign of the past tense, *bá*, *when followed* by a connecting clause, conjunctively defines the time, and corresponds to the English conjunction, when, thus, *go hu sa li thi bá hu ma bám ne*, *when* I arrived at his house, he was not at home; and similarly in the future, *thi sho bá ma bám na pú*, *when* I shall arrive, he may, perhaps, not be at home.

4.—*Of Interjections.*

The following are some of the Interjections.

á-tsa; *á-tsa á-yo*; *á-tsá*; *á-tsá á-yá*; *á-tso*; *á-ya*, are exclamations of vexation, pain, &c. ah! oh! &c.

---

* The sign of the future Participle Definite *sa*, may be, in fact, considered to be the particle of Declension affixed to the Participle Noun, and as a Conjunction bearing an extended meaning, as exemplified under head of Postpositions (Pages 79, 80).

á-yá á-yá; *á-yá-ko*; *á-tse*; *á-tse á*; *á-tse ĩ*, are exclamations denoting surprise, wonder, also pain, &c.

á-chu, an exclamation expressive of cold.

ot-ta-dyól, an exclamation of fright, on being startled.

á-pá-pá, *á-po-po*, exclamations of wonder, astonishment; Gramercy!

á-chhik-ka, an exclamation of disgust; fie! tush! faugh!

bá, is an ejaculation betokening vivacity, impatience, &c., thus, *bá go n͠gak sho*, hold! bah! I'll look to it, I'll do it.

há, a respond on being called; eh! hullo!

róng-nga róng-nga, an expression of grief, sorrow, lamentation; alas! alack! woe! &c.

lá-má khyen no, an exclamation implying grief, wonder, amazement, &c. (It is derived from the Tibetan བླ་མ་མཁྱེན་ནོ *bla-ma mkhyen no*, the Priest knows.)

o-she o-she. *ko-chhe ko-chhe*, are deprecatory exclamations, do not, pray do not, forbear, mercy, &c.

á-chhú-le, is an exclamation of admiration, praise, joy, &c. hurrah! bravo! well done! &c.

PART V.

PARTS OF SPEECH.

Formative and Derivative.—Etymology.

Numeration, &c.

1st.—of Formatives and Derivatives.

The verb is the most simple form of the Parts of Speech, and is the root from which very many of the Nouns, and most of the Adjectives and Adverbs are formed.

The Conjugation of verbs has already been shown; it may be here meet to connote some of the

Verbal affixes and diverse Formatives.

The Conditional

is formed, by the affixed Particle *gang*, thus, *go li gang*, if I speak, *hu thi sho gang*, if he should arrive. Both the protasis and apodosis, of a Conditional sentence, may be connected by means of the above suffix, with the addition of the emphatic Particle *la*, thus, *gang la*, even if; also by *go-rúng*, though, however; so, (or,) *un go ka-do sa ma-zu fan shang ká byi gang la* (or *go-rúng*) *á-gó ma nyin na gang, shú phán-to la ma nyin ne*, and though I give my body to be burned, and (yet) have not charity, it profiteth me nothing.

Contingency

is expressed by the Particle *pú*, as explained under head of Conjugation, so, *so-nóng yu pú*, it may, perhaps, snow. Forms of

Precatives

have also been given under the same head, thus, *bo le*, please give me; *á-bá nun po che*, prithee depart hence; *ná yá*, do let us go; *zúk ka che*, pray let it be done.

Optatives

may be formed, by affixing the Particle *á*, with, or without the reduplication of the final consonant of the verb, thus, *hu mák á*, or, *mák ka á*, may he die. An Optative may also be rendered by the Imperative sign, thus, *pa-no re bám ma o*, let, or may the king live.

Interrogatives

may be expressed by the Particle *a*, so, *hó á-lom li a*, did you say so? *so yu wung a*, is it raining? *hó sa-thá khya shang a*, when will you arrive? (See also under head of *gó*, and *go*, pages 52, 53).

Dubiousness,

or ignorance of a circumstance, may be implied, generally, in the form of Interrogation, by the affixed Particle *te*, thus, *shú zúk ka te*, what can be done; *pa-no kup sa-bá nun thop te*, whence can we obtain a prince?

Potentials

may be formed by such verbs as, *khu*, implying, to be able, so, *zúk khu*, to be able to do; *go khu gang zúk sho*, if I could, I would.

Desideratives

may be expressed by the verb, *gát*, to wish, as, *go nóng gát*, I want to go.

Obligatory Verbs

may be rendered, by adding to the Desiderative, the Substantive verb *nyi*, thus, *gát nyi*, it is necessary, *hláp gát nyi*, it is necessary to learn; (or,) *she-ráp thop shang hláp pung gát nyi*, (or, *gát tung nyi*), to obtain wisdom, learning is necessary.

Causal Verbs

are formed, in some instances, by the addition of *kya*, to the simple verb, thus, *thór*, to escape, *thyór*, to cause to escape; *thóp*, to knock down, *thyóp*, to cause to knock down; *pok*, to cast down, to depose, *pyok*, to cause to cast down, to cause to depose.

When a verb ending in *ng*, takes this causal, the final is changed to *n*; thus, *hróng*, to ascend, *hryón*, to cause to ascend; *dang*, to run, *dyan*, to fling away, (literally, to cause to flee).

When a verb, composed of the consonant *na*, assumes this causal form, the *na*, is changed to *nya*, thus, *nóng*, to go, *nyón*, to cause to go; *nák*, to straighten, *nyák*, to cause to straighten, to rectify.

But this form is not common. The usual mode, of expressing the causal, is by affixing the verb *kón*, to permit, to cause, (as stated under head of conjugation), thus, *buk*, to beat, *buk kón*, to cause to beat; *zúk kón*, to cause to work, &c.

A Causal may also be expressed by means of

Transitive Verbs,

formed by adding, *mát*, to make, to do, — to an Intransitive verb rendered adverbially, thus, *klyám*, to be sweet, *klyám la mát*, to sweeten; *tóm*, to be strong, to be firm, *tóm la mát*, to strengthen; *gó*, to be glad, *gó la mát*, to gladden, &c.

Some verbs such as, *nyón*, causal of *nóng*, to go; *hryón*, causal of *hróng*, to rise, ascend; *byi*, to give; *dyan*, to cast away; and such like, are often affixed to other verbs, giving an emphatic Transitive sense, thus, *óp*, to discharge, (as, arrow, gun), *óp nyón*, to fire off; *tsún*, to lift, *tsún hryón*, to lift up; *dun*, to tell, *dun byi*, to tell to, to relate; *ryák*, to expel, *ryák byi*, to cast out; *póng*, to renounce, *póng dyan*, to renounce altogether, to cast off, &c.

Some Compound verbs, bearing the sense of each verb, convey a modified signification, thus, *bu di*, to bring, from *bu*, to carry, and *di*, to come, to proceed, *bu nóng*, to take away; *hláp*, to learn, *hláp byi*, to teach. The last is, an example of, a neuter verb, changed to a (compound) transitive.

Acquisatives

may be formed by combining, with a verb, the verb *nóng*, to go, or, *ngún*, to become, thus, *hrú*, to be hot, *hrú nóng*, to become hot; *hyang*, to be cold, *hyang ngún*, to become cold, *hyang ngún nón*, it has become cold.

Inceptives

are formed by words implying, to commence, such as, *ayit*, *jeng*, *tsún*, *tsám*, &c. *ayit*, means to create; *jeng*, to found; *tsún*, to lift; and all imply to begin. These generally precede the principal verb, thus, *ayit rok hláp*, to commence to learn to read; *jeng zúk*, to begin to work; this is, however, merely an elliptical form of the Conjunctive Particle, and may be expressed in full, thus, *ayok tsún lung zúk*, to commence work, *á-lang ren tsám lung pi*, commencing, from the present time, to write, *ring chho ál tsám lung tsát-dúng*, to take up and propound a new thesis.

Frequentatives

may be expressed by the repetition of the verb, thus, *zúk zúk*, to work and work, to work often, also continuously.

Continuatives

may, likewise, be formed by the Compound verb *bu nóng*, to carry on, thus,— *tyuk*, to jump, *tyuk bu nóng*, to go jumping along, *pi*, to write, *pi bu no*, continue, follow on the writing, *ayok zúk bu no*, carry on the work. Persistence may also be rendered by the reduplication of the verb, expressed adverbially and with the aid of another verb, thus, *hryóp*, to cry, *hryóp la hryóp la mát*, to weep much and long—or similarly, by the Conjunctive Participle, thus, *dik lung dik lung thuk*, to effect by continuous striving.

Habitude

may be expressed by the addition of the verb, *mát*, thus, *chi*, any fermented or spiritous liquor, *thang*, to drink, *chi than mát*, to be in the habit of drinking beer or spirits; *kháp-chóng li*, to tell lies, *kháp-chóng li mát*, to be in the habit of lying.

Completives

may be expressed by the verb, *lel*,* to be finished, *pi lel*, to finish writing.

Of Abstract Nouns.

Abstract Nouns may be formed, by affixing to the verb, the Particle *lat*, thus, *nók*, to be black, *nók lat*, blackness; *tóm*, to be firm, *tóm lat*, firmness; *ál*, to be new, to be fresh, *ál lat*, newness, freshness; *shóm*, to be stale, *shóm lat*, staleness; *rú*, to be old, worn, *rú lat*, oldness, wear; *jon*, to be young, *jon lat*, youth; *gán*, to be old, *gán lat*, oldness, old age; *nu*, to dare, to presume, *nu lat*, presumption.

lóm, (literally, road, way), may be, sometimes, used to form nouns, thus, *hyók*, to have intercourse with, *hyók lóm*, intercourse; *mát*, to do,

---

* *lel*, is also a Potential, implying, to be able; but in colloquy is seldom used in this sense.

mát lóm, conduct. It may, also, be affixed to a Substantive, forming an abstract noun, thus, *pun-jum*, an enemy, *pun-jum lóm*, enmity. Likewise to a compound noun, thus, *ayeng*, a younger brother, *zang*, like unto, after the manner of, *ayeng zang*, a friend, *ayeng zang lóm*, friendship.

lu, an affix, implying, mode, way of, may also form such nouns as embrace the above sense, for instance, *lik*, to call, *lóm*, to walk; *go hu sa lik lu sa lóm lu thyák*, I recognised his voice and walk, (mode of calling and walking); *dyam*, to dress, *dyam lu*, mode of dressing = fashion; *mát*, to do, *mát lu*, mode of doing = way, habit, custom, &c.

Some nouns may be formed from verbs, by prefixing the vowel *á*, thus, *gó*, to love, *á-gó*, love; *gye*, to conquer, *á-gye*, victory; *thop*, to obtain, *á-thop*, acquisition; *thi*, to arrive, *á-thit*, arrival, &c.

Sometimes other syllables are prefixed, thus, *kryóng*, to praise, *ta-kryóng*, praise, commendation; *thyám*, to arrange, *pa-thyám*, arrangement, adjustment; *sa*, to be well, *ta-sa*, well, health; *cha*, to annoy, to vex, *nung-cha*, annoyance, vexation; *klák*, to revolve, circumvent, *ta-klák*, a revolution, a cycle, a circuit; *dóp*, to be precipitous *rung-dóp* a precipitous place.

In the conversion from verb to noun, the sense, sometimes, becomes modified, thus, *túng*, to lean, to rest upon, *pa-túng*, a walking stick; *ngo*, to be old, *ta-ngot*, grey hairs, (symbolical of old age), &c.

As may be perceived in the last example, some nouns, formed from verbs ending in a vowel, assume a final consonant. Advertence, to this subject, will be hereafter made.

The Participle form, both Present and Future, may be expressed as nouns, thus, *li*, to speak, *li wung*, the words, the speech; *mát*, to do, *mát tung*, the deed ; *mák*, to die, *mák shang thór lyáng ma nyin ne*, there is no escape from death.

This form may be rendered more definite, by the addition of the Article *re*, or the Plural sign, thus, *lók*, to expend, *lók kung re*, the expenditure; *hlók*, to be in excess, *hlók kung re*, the excess, the surplus; *mák kung re*, the mortality, *mák shang pang*, mortals.

It may be also observed, that *mák shang*, which was, in the former example, a Subjective noun, in the latter, changes to an Objective noun.

The Infinitive, (the root of the verb), alone, may often be used to represent the noun, especially in combination with the afore-mentioned Particles, thus, *thi*, to arrive, *thi re*, the arrival ; *nyi*, to have, to possess, *nyi pang*, the possessions ; *lik*, to call, *hó ka-su lik ma thyo nung a*, did you not hear my call ?

There are other modes of expressing words substantively, thus,—

Nouns may be formed from verbs by affixing the word *shet*, which implies, strength, power, also ; for, on account of, thus, *tsám*, to hold, *tsám shet*, the handle, the purchase ; *li*, to speak, *lin shet*, the means of speaking, the tongue ; *ngán*, to sit, *ngán shet*, an article for sitting on, the seat, &c.

Some verbs may, in themselves, represent Nouns, Adjectives and Adverbs ; thus, *hyop*, to accompany *go hu sa hyop sho*, I shall accompany him, *hyop mát*, to make accompaniment, to accompany, *chho hyop re*, the accompanying book ; *hu sa hyop no o*, go along with him.

The Agentive

is expressed by the affix *bo*, whereby may be formed, the English affixes er, man, &c., thus, *mát*, to do, *mát bo*, a doer; *zúk*, to work, *zúk bo*, a worker; *sót*, to kill, *sót bo*, a slayer; *gán*, to be old, *gán bo*, an old animal, (man or beast); *jin*, to be mad, *jin bo*, a madman; *rok*, to read, *rok bo*, a reader; *phyók*, to sweep, *phyók bo*, a sweeper, &c.

Before *bo*, verbs, ending in a vowel, assume their final consonant, thus, *li*, to speak, *lin bo*, a speaker; *shi*, to see, *shim bo*, a seer, a beholder; *di*, to come, *dit bo*, a comer, &c.

Nouns may also be formed from Adjectives, by affixing to the latter the particle *bo*, thus, *á-ryúm*, good, *á-ryúm bo*, a good one; *á-plang*, above, *á-plang bo*, a higher one, a superior, &c.

bo, may be affixed to the following Particles indicative of the Tense, *bám*, the present; *shum*, the euphonic alteration of the Future (*sho*, or, *shu*; *det*, the emphatic Present Participle sign; thus, *zúk bam bo*, one who is working; *zúk shum bo*, one who will work; *zúk det bo*, one who is working or just about to work; *á-dyut sa á-lon, mik-kráp bám bo sang, mák det bo sa mák nón bo sang, tyang thyu lung dá nyi*, after the battle, the sleepers, the dying and the dead, all lay co-mingled.

It may also be affixed to all Auxiliary and Compound verbs, thus, *zúk kón bo*, one who causes work; *zúk lel bo*, one who has finished working; *zúk khat bo*, one capable of working.

The Particle, *shum bo*, is, very generally, affixed to verbs, forming nouns of agency, thus, *ngot*, to cut, *ngot shum bo*, an instrument for cutting, a cutter; *pi*, to write, *pi shum bo*, material for writing, pens, &c;

bu, to carry, *bu shum bo*, means of carrying, a vehicle; *dá*, to lie, *dá shum bo*, an article for lying on, a couch, &c.

All Agentive formatives may be expressed by affixing to a Substantive, a verb in the Agentive form, thus, *ayok*, work, *ayok mát bo*, a worker, a workman; *mán*, game, *ryák*, to follow after, to pursue, *mán ryák bo*, a hunter; *ngo*, fish, *tsám*, to catch, *ngo tsám bo*, a fisherman; *úl*, to solicit, to beg, *sa-nyim*, alms, charity, *sa-nyim úl bo*, a beggar; *tyu*, to train, to discipline, *on*, a horse, *on tyu bo*, a horse-breaker; *bu*, a load, *bu*, to carry, *bu bun bo*, a porter; *món*, drugs, *ul*, to sell, *món ul bo*, a druggist; *li*, a house, *dók*, to own, *li dók bo*, a house owner; *chho*, a book, *ya*, to know, *chho yam bo*, a scholar; *ring*, a language, *myá*, to be versed in, *ring myám bo*, a linguist; *kár-tsu*, astronomy, (སྐར *skar*, a star, *tsu*, calculation), *myong*, to be skilled, *kár-tsu myong bo*, an astronomer; *nák tsu*, (ནག *nag*, black), black arts, divination, *nák tsu yam bo*, (or, *myám bo*, *myong bo*, &c.), a diviner, a necromancer, &c.

Adjectives

may, in like manner, be formed by the affix *bo*, by which, either simply, or combined with other formatives, the English Adjectives of quality and manner, &c, terminating in able, ible, ful, &c, may be expressed, thus— *ryám*, to be beautiful, *ryám bo*, beautiful; *gán*, to be old, *gán bo*, old, aged; *gyan*, to be troublesome, *gyan bo*, troublesome; *nat*, to hurt, to be injurious, *nat bo*, hurtful, baneful, &c.

And so compound formatives may be expressed, thus, *kóm*, silver, money, *nyi*, to have, to possess, *kóm nyim bo*, a possessor of money, wealthy; *shet*, strength, *shet nyim bo*, strong, vigorous; *kho*, use, profit, *kho nyim bo*, useful, profitable; *kher*, skilfulness, dexterity, *kher nyim bo*, skilful, dextrous; *rang*, to watch, to guard, *ran bo*, watchful, *ka-jú*, a dog, *ka-jú ran bo*, a watch dog; *li*, to speak, *ya*, to know, *lin yam bo*, talkative; *lin myám bo*, eloquent; *on*, a horse, *thúl*, to ride, *on thúl bo*, a rider, a horseman; *jong*, to be accustomed, to be practised in, *on thúl jóng bo*, an experienced equestrian, &c.

Passive Adjectives

may be formed, from Active verbs, by affixing *thóm bo*, the agentive of the verb *tho*, to place; thus, *li*, to speak, *li thóm bo*, spoken; *pi*, to write, *pi thóm bo*, written; *zúk*, to make, *zúk thóm bo*, made, fashioned; *fat*, earth, *fat zúk thóm bo*, made of earth, earthen, *fyu*, a cooking vessel, *fyu fat zúk thóm bo*, an earthen cooking vessel; *thók*, to weave, *thók thóm bo*, woven, *tór*, silk, *tór thók thóm bo*, woven silk; *yuk*, a letter, *tho*, to register, *yuk tho thóm bo*, a registered letter, &c.

Adjectives may, also, be expressed by verbs in the Participle form, in conjunction with the relative Particle *sa*; thus, *ro*, to fear, *lóm*, a road, *ro wung sa lóm*, a fearful road; *thyan*, to laugh, *thyan nung sa ayok*, a laughable affair; *mák*, to die, *dak*, illness, *mák shang sa dak*, a mortal disease; *byóng*, to coax, *óng kup*, a child, *byóng ngung sa óng kup*, a coaxing, winsome child; *zo*, to eat, *thám-pót*, a fruit, *zo shum bo sa thám-pót*, an edible fruit; *óng-chhi*, oppression, *ka bo*, an overseer of work, *óng-chhi mát tung sa ka bo*, an oppressive task-master.

Nouns and Substantives may, in like manner, be rendered Adjectively; thus, *yu-muk*, mourning, lamentation, *yu-muk sa á-tyan*, a mournful, lamentable occurrence; *kúng*, wood, *rom*, a box, *kúng sa rom*, a box of wood, a wooden box; *pun-jeng*, iron, *ta-rol*, a bar, *pun-jeng sa ta-rol*, an iron bar; *fat sa fyu*, an earthen cooking vessel.

This form may be expressed elliptically, thus, *kúng rom*, a wooden box; *pun-jeng ta-rol*, an iron bar; *fat fyu*, an earthen cooking vessel, *gál*, to break, *fat fyu gál thóm bo*, a broken earthen cooking vessel, &c., &c.

Nouns and Verbs, &c.

are occasionally formed by a compound of two words, some of which may be used separately, and some only in composition; thus, *thám*, a thing, is prefixed to a number of words. It generally gives a modified sense to the affixed word, though in some instances, the latter, in a disconnected state, may bear altogether a different meaning, or may not be employed in Lepcha; so, *pót*, to fructify, *thám-pót*, a fructified thing, (*á-pót*), a fruit; *bang*, (*á-bang*), a foundation, a stem, *tham-bang*, a support, the produce of the earth, &c.; *chang*, to foster, *thám-chang*, a quadruped, animals inferior to (claiming the cherishment of) man; *bik*, means a cow, but, *thám-bik*, implies, an insect. *so*, rain, 2, the weather, 3, (in compos.) the state of the weather or atmosphere; *sóng*, to be clear, to be pure, *so-sóng* the morning dawn; *myar*, dim, obscurity, *so-myar*, the shades of evening; *lyóp*, to flash, *so-lyóp*, sheet-lightning. *sák* (in compos.), the mind and its state, *ryú*, to be good, *sák-ryú*, to rejoice; *tóp*, to support, *sák-tóp*, to uphold the mind, to encourage, to comfort. *lót*, to return; prefixed gives signification of repetition, corresponding to the English particle *re;* thus, *zúk*, to make, *lót zúk*, to re-make; *thop*, to obtain, *lót thop*, to recover; *byi*, to give, *lót byi*, to restore, &c., &c.

Nouns of Magnitude

may be expressed by the affixed Particle *mo*, (*á-mo*, mother), so— *li*, a house, *li mo re*, the large house; *rung-nyit úng*, the river Rung-nyit, *rung-nyit úng mo*, the great Rung-nyit river, &c. Affixed to verbs of magnitude and quality, it forms

Nouns, Adjectives, and Adverbs of Intensity,

thus—*gyáp*, to be much, to be numerous; *ti*, to be large, to be great; *gyáp mo*, very much, very numerous; *ti mo*, very large, very great; *tun-rot-pót á-tyúm ti mo sa gyáp mo tyúl ngán*, the grapes hung in large and numerous clusters; *go gyáp mo shi*, I saw numbers; *hum gyáp mo byi*, give him much, plentifully; abundance.

A Patrial

is formed, by affixing *mo*, to the name of the country, thus—*pat*, Tibet, *pat mo*, a Tibetan; *prú*, Butan, *prú-mo*, a Butian, or, (as commonly called) a Butia; *phi-ling*, Europe, *phi-ling mo*, an European, &c.*

---

* Observe *mo*, as a particle of magnitude, with the Latin suffix ***supre-mo***, ***extre-mo***, ***pri-mo***, ***ulti-mo***, &c.; also Sax. *ma*, more; *mæst*, *mo*-est = most, &c., &c.

This *mo*, is simply the basic creative *m*, (See *m*, and *Diagram* in Powers of Letters,) with the vowel affixed. In Lepcha, *m*, in itself forms one of the substantive verbs, is, am, was; (it means also, to pray, synonymous with, to create, to make; "ask and ye shall receive;" whence Lep· *mo*, = ***á-mo***, = Heb. אם *ám*, *a mother*, (Eng. *am*, [being]) ; (so Lat. *a-mo* love, the flow that engenders [itself], produces, makes). In Tib. མ *m* represents an indefinite article, a, an, (being, matter); likewise, the capital, the stock, (the *Source*, whence all floweth); hence also, mother. In Sanskrit मा *má*, means, to create, to produce, also, mother. Arabic ما *má*, water, semen, a mother, (productive flow); Persian ما *má*, we, (beings); Lepcha

Nouns of Diminutiveness

are formed, by the affix *kup*, (*á-kup*, a child, little); so, *li kup*, a small house, a cottage; *fyu kup*, a pipkin; *óng*, a child, *óng kup*, a little child; *rung-nyit úng kup*, the little Rung-nyit river. Like *mo*, it may be affixed to a verb, implying minuteness, forming and giving emphasis to

---

mo, a female, (sex); Chin. 母 *mo*, mother; Sax. moder, Lat. mater, (μήτρα a womb); mulier &c.; a genitrix; (so, milk, the flow and power of *m*, productive force flowing from the *μαμμα*, the productive source; see *l*, *k*, &c. in P. of L.) The word *man* is compounded of above creative *m* with the basic formative *n*, flowing with primitive force; hence *man* (Chin. 民 *min* men,) simply signifies, the created being; emphatically, above all other *ani-ma*. It was formerly, like the Lepcha *ma-ró*, applied to either sex; so *he-man*, *she-man*, &c.; so also *wo-man*, (root, Lep. *w*, to be worthy, worth; Privative, Sax. *wa*, sorrow, woe, ("in sorrow shalt thou bring forth children"); Sansk. वे we, to weave; Sax. *wefan*, to weave; *wef*, *wif*, a woman, a wife, = a weaver; so Lep. *wo-mo*, a spindle, a spinning-wheel,—symbolical of the flow of the life, and work of a woman. Sax. wer, a man (the primeval flow of w,) is applied to the male; (see *w*, *r*, &c. in Powers of Letters).

The same word *man* is seen flowing with privative force in the Lep. *mán*, to wan, to want, to be minus, adverb, no, not; Sansk. मा *má*, no, not, *non;* Heb. מאן *mán*, to refuse, to deny; Arab. مان *mán*, to forbid; Sax. *man*, sin, evil; Lat. *mal*, *malus*, &c. &c. We have it again with primitive power in Sansk. मन *man*, the soul, the spirit, मान *mán*, honor, (honor, literally, flowing with *high*, *living* spirit: privative, Fr. *honi*, evil, dishonor). In Latin we find *mo*, as a suffix to ho, *ho-mo*, signifying man, (not radically, as has been rendered, from *humus* earth-born; but simply born of or created with h, (life). In Chinese *ho*, is a radical, and frequent recurring word, implying a primitive flow, as, 呼 *ho*, to breathe forth; 丂 *ho*, air; 火 *ho*, fire; 喔 *ho*, sound; 河 *ho*, a river, (all flowing forth); 好 *ho*, good, (primitive); 合 *ho*, to unite, (the flow round, the circular flow); 禾 *ho*, grain, (the fuel, the support of life); 血 *ho*, *hue*, blood = (the flow = life), &c. So Heb. הי *hi*, יה *jah*, יהי *ja-hi*, lit. existing, being, (the Being, I *am*); Arab. هو *ho*, *hu*, he is, (the Being); Heb. הוא *hoa*, he, the Being; Arab. هوا *hoa*, the air, (the spirit); Hind. هوا *hoa*, was; هو *ho*, art; هي *hi*, is, (the Being), &c., &c. Take examples of *h* in the pronouns, (the pronouns, primitively, representing the First Being); Lep. *hó* thou, (the Being); Lep. *hu*, Sax. and Eng. he, (the Being); Lep. *hu-s*, (of he), Sax. and Eng. *his*, (the Being's); Inflection, Lep. *hum*, Sax. and Eng. *him;* (Arab. هم *ham*, a mutual flow, [of the Persons]), Sansk. हम *ham*, we (Sax. *hwám*, whom;) Lep. *á-yú*, Sax. *eow* Eng.

Noun, Adjective, and Adverb,

thus— *chu*, to be small, *chu kup re*, the small one, the little one; *zo chu kup n̄yi bám*, there is only a very little rice; *hu chu kup mát ma zo ne*, he only ate very little.*

The Season, or Appropriate time

for anything, is expressed by the suffix *rón*, and may be affixed to Substantives,

---

ye, you; Lep. *hu-yú*, Sax. *heo, hii*, &c. Eng. *they;* Inflect. *hu-yúm*, Sax. *heom*, *hem*, Eng. them; Sax. Gen. *hi-ra*, of them, (relatively, of the being); comparatively, Sax. *heah*, *hiah*, high; *hiera*, higher, (Gr. ἱερός, appertaining to [ἴε, εἰμί the Being] the Gods, [the eternal flow], Lat. *hæres*, the heir, the successor, [the flow on flow]), Ger. *herr*, man, (hon); Sax. *herra*, a lord, Gr. ἥρως, Lat. *heros*, a hero, (emphatically, a man, a being). So we have Arab ماي *mai*, implying extension, Sans. महा *ma-há*, great, (high flow, life), &c. In the Ho language, *ho*, means a man. (For the root and the power of *h*, in these, and in all other words, see *h*, in Powers of Letters.)

The Lepcha word *ma-ró*, is seen flowing with primitive force in the Heb. מרא *mará*, erect (as man), high, exalted, Chaldee *ma-ra*, a great man, (Arab. مير *mir*), a prince, a lord; (Sax. *mere*, Lat. *maris*, *Fr. mer*, [*mere*, mother,] a lake, a sea, (whence the waters [the spirits] flow and return); Hind. ميرا *mera*, mine, (the Lord's). Compare also Lep. *ma-ró*, with the Latin word *mas*, (*ma's*, of or belonging to the being), dropping the *r* and resuming it again in the inflection, *ma-ris*, whence, Mars, martial, &c., so also, *mos*, *mo-ris*, of, or appertaining to the (primitive, the right) way of man = mo-ral, &c. The privative force is at once seen in such words, as Lep. *ma-ri*, dirt, pollution, Sansk. मृ *mri*, मरा *ma-rá*, Lat. *mors*, *mortis*, (μορτός,) of or appertaining to the (μόρος) destiny of man = death; Pers. مرد mard, (prim.) a man; مرده *mur-dah*, (life flown), dead, Eng. murder, &c.; mor-tality. (Note also, *ma-rum*, the allotted period of life; likewise, *ma-ra*, an evil spirit of great malignity [Sans. मृत Gr. μορμώ] whose influence is fatal; so, Heb. מאר a *spreading* evil, [Lev. xiii. 51, ממארת translated, a *fretting* leprosy], מר bitter, Sans. मरु a desert, without water, [without روح spirit, life]; so, Gr. μαραίνω, μάρανσις, a flow to naught, to death; Eng. to mar, murr, murrain, &c., &c.;—see, definition of primitive and privative letters in P. of L.). So also Lep. *m*, negative, privative, not, without; Tib. མ *má*, not, Pers. موا *muá*, dead, (without *a*), Heb. מת *mat*, dead, (without *at*), Arab. موت *mot*, repose, death, (without *ot*), &c. &c.; (see *m*, *&c.* in Powers of Letters).

In making, here, these few desultory observations, it is not my object to give an exposition of the powers of letters, nor would it be possible to do so within the limits of a foot-note; but I hope, shortly, to publish a work, with a diagram, showing the true Powers of Letters; exponential of the basis of all language and tongues.

* *Kup*, a child, a *cub*, &c.

or verbs, thus, *ayok*, work, *ayok rón*, work time; *lyón*, play, *lyón rón*, play time; *pát*, to sow, *pát rón*, sowing time; *ayek*, to reap, *ayek rón*, reaping time, harvest, &c.

Nouns expressing—time, the period of,—may be expressed by the word, *thok*, thus, *óng*, a child, *óng thok*, childhood; *pa-nyóm*, an old man, *pa-nyóm thok ká*, in old age; *mi*, a man, *mi thok*, a generation, a period of one generation. It is also affixed to verbs, in the form of abstract nouns, thus, *zú*, to live, *zúm thok ká*, during lifetime, &c.

Adjectives

expressing worthy, deserving of, fit for, proper, may be formed from verbs by affixing the suffix *chhok*, thus— *lun*, to reprimand, *lun chhok*, fit to be reprimanded, blameworthy, reprehensible; *kryón* to praise, *kryón chhok*, deserving of praise, praiseworthy, commendable; *zo*, to eat, *zóm chhok*, fit for eating, edible.

This form of speech may be also expressed, by the verb *thup*, to be fitting to be admissible, &c., thus, *zóm thup*, admissible food, food fit for eating, &c.; it likewise may be rendered by the particle *shet*, for, on account of, so, *zóm shet*, for eating, edible, (see also, *shet*, p. 97).

Comparative Similitude

may be expressed by the suffix, *zang*, thus, *á-re zang*, like this; *o-re zang*, like that; *á-chu re zang*, like that down there; *á-kup zang*, like a child, childish; *óng zang*, boyish; *ta-ayu zang*, womanish; *ta-gri zang*, manly; *pa-no zang*, king-like, kingly; *so-zang*, cold, *hó so-zang re zang nyóng*, do you feel cold, (literally, after the manner of cold).

External Resemblance

may be indicated by the particle *mu,* thus, *dak,* to be sick, *dak mu,* sickly; *mák mu,* deathlike; *zóm mu,* an eatable appearance, palatable looking, &c.

From Substantives, derived from the Tibetan, Adjectives of intensity, expressing possession, fulness, &c., may be formed by the addition of the particles, *chen,* and *den,* (derived from the Tibetan adjective formatives, ཅན *chen,* ལྡན *ldan*), thus, *nor,* wealth, *nor-den,* rich, wealthy; *rin chen,* valuable, costly; *nóng chen,* (སྣང་ཅན *snang-chan,* full of light) invaluable, very precious; *ú-chen,* headed character, (དབུ་ཅན *dbu chan,* large Tibetan character). A superlative may be formed by the suffix *chhok,* as explained under head of Degrees of Comparison, (page 32), &c.

2nd.—Of Negation.

The negative, no, is expressed by, *má ne,* *mán,* *mán ne,* as stated under head of Adverbs.

A verb is expressed negatively by prefixing the particle, *ma,* and affixing *ne*; thus, *ya,* to know, *ma ya ne,* not to know; *shi,* to see, *ma shi ne,* not to see; *són,* to be dry, *ma són ne,* not to be dry.

Verbs ending in a vowel, may generally have a negative *n* surposed ni addition to the one affixed, thus, *nyi,* to be, to have, *ma nyin ne,* not to be, not to have; *khu,* to be able, *ma khun ne,* not to be able.

When a verbal Particle forms part of the sentence, it follows the negative sign, and the *ne* becomes changed to *na,* thus, *go ma nóng na bám*, I am not going, *hu ma nóng na sho*, he will not go; *hu ma nóng na shang a*, will he not go? &c.

In the employment however of the present participle, the negative particle is incorporated in the participle sign; thus, *li wung*, speaking, *ma li nung*, not speaking; *mát tung*, doing, *ma mát nung*, not doing.

Another negative particle is expressed by, *num*. This appears to be a coalesced form of the particles *ma*, *na*; thus, *go pi ma o*, I am writing, *go ma pi num o*, I am not writing, or, I shall not write, (instead of *ma pi na ma o*, which would be long and inelegant); *kyón dit ma nyin nung ma go num o*, it is not that I am wanting in compassion. *num o*, may be affixed to the negative Adverb, without the intervention of the verb, thus, *má num o*, not so, by no means.

A Negative Agentive

may be rendered by affixing *bo*, to the preceding particle, *num*, united to a verb; this forms nouns and adjectives of negation, represented in English by the prefixed particles *un*, *in*, *ir*, &c.; thus, *jóng*, to be experienced, *ma jóng num bo*, an inexperienced person, inexperienced; *fa-lyeng ma jóng num bo*, an inexperienced youth; *khu*, to be able; *ma khun num bo*, unable, impracticable; *ma thup num bo*, improper; *ma lyok num bo*, unlike; *ma zak num bo*, incorrect; *á-tyan*, an occurrence, *á-tyan ma ryú num bo*, an unlucky event, an inauspicious, unpropitious occurrence; *chik*, to measure, measurement, *chik ma khun num bo*, immeasurable; *kṛin so*, gratitude, *kṛin so ma ya num bo*, not to know gratitude, ungrateful;

krút, counsel, *chhóm*, to agree, *krút ma chhóm num bo*, not agreeing in counsel, dissentient, &c.

The English privative particle "less", &c., is particularly expressed by affixing to a noun, *ma nyin num bo*, one not possessing, without; thus, *á-bo ma nyin num bo*, without a father, fatherless; *á-kup ma nyin num bo*, childless; *grón ma nyin num bo*, hopeless; *chhet*, strength, *chhet ma nyin num bo*, without strength, feeble, &c.

An Adjective

signification may be given, by affixing the particle *sa*, to the Negative Participle, thus, *kho*, to be useful, *ma kho nung sa thám*, or, *kho ma nyin nung sa thám*, a worthless article.

Adverbs of Negation

may be formed by affixing *ma nyin ne*, to the affirmatives, thus, *sa-thá la*, *shok na la*, ever, *sa-thá la ma nyin ne*, *shok na la ma nyin ne*, never; *sa-bá la ma nyin ne*, no where; *to la ma nyin ne*, no one; *shú la ma nyin ne*, nothing; *sa-re la ma nyin ne*, no way, no means, no manner, &c.

Verbs in the negative form, may be used adverbially, thus, *chhet*, to stop, to cease, *ma chhet ne*, not to cease; *so yu*, to rain, *so ma chhet na yu*, to rain without ceasing, incessantly; *ro*, to fear, *ma ro na nóng*, to go along fearlessly; this form may be more fully expressed by adding the conjunctive participle sign; or the Auxiliary verb, *mát*, may be introduced, thus, *ma ching na lung zúk*, or, *ma ching na mát zúk*, to work or do anything without thinking, thoughtlessly.

Negation is emphatically expressed, by the adverbial particle *la*, affixed to the verb, and a repetition of the latter in the negative ; thus, *go bám la ma bám ne*, I shall not remain at all ; *go nóng la ma nóng ne*, I shall certainly not go, nothing shall induce me to go, &c.

Verbs compounded of two syllables, when expressed negatively, the syllables are separated by tmesis ; the negative particles being affixed to the final syllable ; thus, *mik-kráp*, to sleep, *mik ma kráp ne*, not to sleep ; *kyón-dyak*, to pity, *kyón ma dyak ne*, not to pity ; *sák-ching*, to think, *sák ma ching ne*, not to think ; *den-ri*, to believe, *den ma ri ne*, not to believe.

But this disconnection does not take place, when the dissyllabic word is a substantive, or a verb rendered as a noun, and governed by another verb ; the negative particles would, in this case, be affixed to the governing verb ; thus, (or,) *kyón-dyak* (or, *kyón-dit*) *ma ya ne*, not to know compassion, to be heartless, pitiless, merciless ; *sák-chin ma khun num bo*, one unable to think, a fool, an idiot, &c.

The negative is, sometimes, expressed by either one of the two particles singly, or, as before remarked, a negative particle may be surposed ; thus, *ma ya*, or, *ma yan*, don't know ; *ma khun*, can't, impossible ; *ma shin*, can't see ; *mát ma mát*, doing or not doing ; *mák na mák, zú na zú*, dying or not dying, living or dead.

A form of negation was expressed by affixing to the verb the particle *ta-o ;* thus, *go á-re zang sa thám móng myón ta-o*, I would not dream of such a thing. This form, though sometimes found in books, would, now, be very rarely used in colloquy.

The Tibetan Negative

particle ᰕᰬᰳ *met*, (མེད *med*), is sometimes affixed to verbs derived from the Tibetan ; thus, ᰍᰨᰵ ᰕᰬᰳ *nóng-met*, without value, valueless, (from སྣང་མེད *snang med*, destitute of light); ᰌᰨᰭ ᰕᰬᰳ *dók-met*, (བདག་མེད *bdag med*), without an owner, ownerless; ᰣᰪ ᰕᰬᰳ *ú-met*, (དབུ་མེད *dbu med*, without a head, headless), the small Tibetan character.

The Negative Imperative

is formed, by changing the affixed particle ᰍᰬ *ne*, into ᰍᰪᰰ *nun ;* thus, ᰕ ᰜᰧ ᰍᰪᰰ *ma li nun*, do not speak ; ᰕ ᰛᰨ ᰍᰪᰰ *ma ro nun*, do not fear.

When the verb ends in a consonant, the final may be reduplicated and embodied in the negative postposition, or it is optional not to do so ; thus, ᰕ ᰕᰦᰳ ᰊᰪᰰ *ma mát tun*, or, ᰕ ᰕᰦᰳ ᰍᰪᰰ *ma mát nun*, do not, don't ; ᰕ ᰈᰨᰭ ᰀᰪᰰ *ma jók kun*, do not make a noise ; ᰕ ᰝᰥᰤᰨᰱ ᰎᰪᰰ *ma hryóp pun*, do not cry ; ᰕ ᰋᰵ ᰅᰪᰰ *ma thang ngun*, do not drink, &c. ; or, ᰍᰪᰰ *nun*, may, at pleasure, be used with all ; the reduplication of the final, however, is in general to be preferred.

3rd.—Of Inflection.

There is not much inflection in the Lepcha language, but some words, when transmuted from verb to noun, or adjective, or before certain particles and auxiliary verbs, undergo a degree of change.

Substantive nouns are uninflected by number or case. The form of inflection, in the declension of pronouns, has been given under the head of pronouns.

Verbs, ending in a vowel, when changed to the simple form of adjectives, by the addition of the prefix ᰣᰦ *á*, invariably, (when capable of final inflection), assume the final *m*; thus, *sú*, to be hot, to be pungent, *á-súm*, hot, pungent; (see also under head of adjectives, pages 30, 31).

All verbs are not inflected, (as exemplified in pages 31 and 47), but such as do take inflection, take it before auxiliary verbs, (not indicative of tense), such as *khu*, to be able; *lel*, to be finished; *gát*, to desire; *mát*, to make, to do, &c. Also before particles and words forming adjectives and nouns of agency, manner, place, &c., as *bo*, *lat*, *lu*, *lyáng*, *&c.*

Nouns or formative adjectives, formed from verbs ending in a vowel, when inflected, may assume either of the three (3) finals, *m*, *n*, or *t*, according as custom or a regard to euphony may have prescribed. Nouns generally take the last mentioned final, only a very few, formed with the prefixed *á*, possess the final *n*, (not including such as are derived from verbs ending in *ng*).

The following are examples—

Verb.	Adjective.	Noun.
shú, to be fat,	*á-shúm*, fat,	*á-shút*, fat.
ryú, to be good,	*á-ryúm*, good,	*sák-ryút*, pleasure, cheerfulness.
di, to come,	*á-dim*, coming,	*á-dit*, a coming. *sák-á-dim*, pleasure, satisfaction.
tsú, to boil,	*á-tsúm*, boiling,	*sák-tsúm*, ebullition of spirits, gaiety, hilarity.
a, to be warm,	*á-am*, warm,	*á-am*, warmth.
thi, to arrive,	*thit bo*, Ag. arriver,	*á-thit*, arrival.
dyu, to fight,	*dyut bo*, a fighter,	*á-dyut*, war, battle.
tu, to be ominous,	*tum bo*, ominous,	*á-tum*, the evil effect of the omen.

ru, to be far,	*ma-rum*, far, sometimes *á-rum*,	*ma-rum*, far, afar.
hrú, to be hot,	*á-hrúm*, hot,	*á-hrún*, heat.

Further inflection takes place, in the change from *o*, to *ó*, and from *ng*, to *n*. The following are examples:—

Change from *o*, to *ó*.

zo, to eat,	*zóm bo*, Adj. eating, Ag. eater,	*á-zóm*, food.
tho, to place,	*thóm bo*, Adj. placing, Ag. placer.	*thóm-lat*, location, installation.
bo, to give,	*bón bo*, Adj. giving, Ag. giver.	*bón lat*, the giving, donation, gift.

Exceptions.

so, to convey,	*so bo*, Ag. conveyer,	*so lat*, conveyance, vehicle.
ro, to fear,	*rom bo*, Adj. fearful, Ag. fearer,	*rom lat*, fear, dread.
klo, to fall,	*klom bo*, a faller.	*klom lu*, manner of falling.

Change from *ng*, to *n*.

thang, to drink,	*than bo*, a drinker,	*á-than*, drink.
rang, to watch,	*ran bo*, a watcher,	*ran lu*, mode of watching.
dang, to run,	*dan bo*, a runner,	*dan lyáng*, means of, or place for running.
klóng, to send,	*klón bo*, a sender,	*klón lóm*, way of sending.
lóng, to lead,	*lón bo*, a leader,	*lón khu*, to be able to lead.

lyáng, to hand round,	*chi lyán bo*, cup-bearer,	*lyán lel*, handed round, distributed.
dóng, to search,	*dón bo*, a searcher,	*dón shet*, means of searching.
ryáng, to crow, (as a cock),	*hik ryán bo*, a cock that crows,	*á-ryán*, the crow of a cock.

Exceptions.

myong, to be versed in,	*myong bo*, one versed in.
jóng, to be accustomed to,	*jóng bo*, one accustomed.
hóng, to be low,	*hóng bo*, hollow.
sóng, to be endowed with,	*sóng bo*, endowed with.
shong, to dry, &c.	*shong lyáng*, a drying place.

All verbs, capable of final inflection, assume their special inflection, when preceded by the adjective, and nominal particle *á;* but all verbs that bear inflection, do not necessarily take this prefixed *á;* thus, the verbs *li*, to speak; *shi*, to see; *tho*, to place; *dú*, to dig; *byi*, to give, &c.; may all be inflected, as, *shim khu*, to be able to see; *thóm lyáng*, a place for placing on, a rest; *dún jóng bo*, one accustomed to dig; *byin bo*, a giver, &c. In such verbs, the *á*, could not be correctly prefixed, *á-byin*, *á-shim*, &c., would not be idiomatic. An exception occurs in *li*, to speak, for though *á-lin*, would not be accurate, *á-li*, is so; the sense, however, becomes modified to the instrument of speech—the tongue.

Inflection is not affected by the intervention of a word or words between the inflected and inflecting verb; thus, *li*, to speak, *lin khu*, to be able to speak, *lin ma khun ne*, to be unable to speak; *lin ma ta ne*, not to dare to speak; *lin á-gyáp mát bo*, one who speaks much; *dang*, to run, *dan chóng khum bo*, one able to run swiftly, &c.

Inflection does not take place in verbs that are directly derived from the Tibetan; thus, *jú*, to sit, *jú bo*, a sitter, (never *jún bo*), &c.

No inflection takes place before verbs or particles indicative of tense, or voice, or that bear merely a transitive sense, nor before the particles of declension, ordinary postpositive particles, or the adverbial particle *la;* thus, *li byi*, to tell; *klóng nyón*, to send off; *tho ayat*, to place down, to leave off, to leave alone; *shi thóm bo*, the thing seen, the view; *ro nun*, through fear; *zo sa*, for eating, &c. (Not, *lin byi; klón nyón; thóm ayát; shim thóm bo; rom nun; zóm sa;* unless the two latter were altered to nouns, then, *á-rom nun; á-zóm sa*, would be correct).

An exception to this rule is met with in the particle *det;* verbs, ending in a vowel, are inflected before it; thus, *lin det*, speaking, or just about to speak; *dit det*, coming, or just about to come. (No other verb or particle, representative of the tense, such as *bám, ngán, sho, fát, shang, lung*, &c., occasions inflection. The verb *kón*, [before which inflection takes place], is indicative of the imperative *mood*, and is an auxiliary verb similar to *khu, lel, &c*).

Also before the verb *nóng*, to go, no inflection takes place; *nón*, forming a past tense, as, *hu thi nón*, he arrived, of course does not inflect, and though sometimes acting apparently as an auxiliary verb; as, *go zúk nóng sho*, I shall go and do it; *hum li nón*, went to speak to him; it is in fact independent of the preceding verb, the sentence being elliptical, as explained in page 51.

The above are rules for inflection and non-inflection, as far as can be laid down. A little observation and practice will soon enable the learner to acquire the knowledge of what words do, or do not take inflection.

4.—*Of Numeration.*

The Lepcha Numerals are similar to the Tibetan. The figures, and the written denominations, are as follows:

Cardinal Numbers.

1 ᱁ ᰀᰦᰳ *kát*, one.
2 ᱂ ᰉᰳ *nyat*, two.
3 ᱃ ᰠᰦᰮ *sám*, three.
4 ᱄ ᰑᰜᰧ *fa-li*, four.
5 ᱅ ᰑᰅᰨ *fa-ngo*, five.
6 ᱆ ᰊᰛᰭ *ta-rak*, six.
7 ᱇ ᰀᰀᰤᰭ *ka-kyak*, seven.
8 ᱈ ᰀᰀᰪ *ka-ku*, eight.
9 ᱉ ᰀᰀᰤᰨᰳ *ka-kyót*, nine.
10 ᱁᱀ ᰀᰊᰧ *ka-ti*, ten.

Eleven, twelve and the 'teens are expressed by affixing ᰋᰦᰱ *tháp*, to the digits, combined with ᰀᰊᰧ *ka-ti*, ten, thus,

11 ᱁᱁ ᰀᰊᰧ ᰀᰦᰳ ᰋᰦᰱ *ka-ti kát tháp*, eleven.
12 ᱁᱂ ᰀᰊᰧ ᰉᰳ ᰋᰦᰱ *ka-ti nyat tháp*, twelve.

This form is generally abbreviated, by leaving out ᰀᰊᰧ *ka-ti*, thus—

13 ᱁᱃ ᰠᰦᰮ ᰋᰦᰱ *sám tháp*, thirteen.
14 ᱁᱄ ᰑᰜᰧ ᰋᰦᰱ *fa-li tháp*, fourteen.
15 ᱁᱅ ᰑᰅᰨ ᰋᰦᰱ *fa-ngo tháp*, fifteen.
16 ᱁᱆ ᰊᰛᰭ ᰋᰦᰱ *ta-rak tháp*, sixteen.
17 ᱁᱇ ᰀᰀᰤᰭ ᰋᰦᰱ *ka-kyak tháp*, seventeen.
18 ᱁᱈ ᰀᰀᰪ ᰋᰦᰱ *ka-ku tháp*, eighteen.
19 ᱁᱉ ᰀᰀᰤᰨᰳ ᰋᰦᰱ *ka-kyót tháp*, nineteen.
20 ᱂᱀ ᰂᰦ ᰀᰦᰳ *khá kát*, twenty, one score.

and so on, adding one, two, &c., and then proceeding on by scores, ᰂᰦ ᰀᰦᰳ ᰠ ᰀᰦᰳ *khá kát sa kát*, twenty-one; ᰂᰦ ᰀᰦᰳ ᰠ ᰉᰳ *khá kát sa nyat*, twenty-two, &c.; ᰂᰦ ᰀᰦᰳ ᰠ ᰀᰊᰧ *khá kát sa ka-ti*, thirty; ᰂᰦ ᰀᰦᰳ ᰠ ᰀᰊᰧ ᰀᰦᰳ ᰋᰦᰱ *khá kát sa ka-ti kát tháp*, or, ᰂᰦ ᰀᰦᰳ ᰠ ᰀᰦᰳ ᰋᰦᰱ *khá kát sa kát tháp*, thirty-one; ᰂᰦ ᰀᰦᰳ ᰠ ᰉᰳ ᰋᰦᰱ *khá kát sa nyat tháp*, thirty-two, &c.; ᰂᰦ ᰉᰳ *khá nyat*, forty; ᰂᰦ ᰉᰳ ᰠ ᰀᰊᰧ *khá nyat sa ka-ti*, fifty, &c.*

---

* This form was of course very cumbersome and awkward, entirely preventing the teaching of ordinary arithmetic. A decimal mode was necessary; which the Lepchas, on being taught, at once saw the advantage of, and learned with avidity. In a school which I established, during the short period I had the opportunity of conducting it, the Lepchas made great progress in arithmetic; and now, on all occasions when counting, they adopt the decimal mode taught them.

For the reason mentioned in the foot note, I altered this mode of reckoning, b y introducing a regular decimal system. *ka*, is an abbreviation of, and stands for *ka-ti*, ten, therefore from ten upwards, the notation may be expressed, *ka kát sa kát*, eleven ; *ka kát sa nyat*, twelve, &c ; *ka kát sa ka-kyót*, nineteen.

20 *ka nyat*, twenty.

21 *ka nyat sa kát*, twenty-one.

22 *ka nyat sa nyat*, twenty-two.

29 *ka nyat sa ka-kyót*, twenty-nine.

30 *ka sám*, thirty.

40 *ka fa-li*, forty.

50 *ka fa-ngo*, fifty.

60 *ka ta-rak*, sixty.

70 *ka ka-kyak*, seventy.

80 *ka ka-ku*, eighty.

90 *ka ka-kyót*, ninety.

100 *gyó kát*, one hundred.

101 *gyó kát sa kát*, one hundred and one.

102 *gyó kát sa nyat*, one hundred and two.

110 *gyó kát sa ka-ti*, one hundred and ten.

111 *gyó kát sa ka kát sa kát*, one hundred and eleven.

120 *gyó kát sa ka nyat*, one hundred and twenty.

130 *gyó kát sa ka sám*, one hundred and thirty.

200 *gyó nyat*, two hundred.

300 *gyó sám*, three hundred.

400 *gyó fa-li*, four hundred.

500 *gyó fa-ngo*, five hundred.

600 ᱆᱀᱀ *gyó ta-rak* six hundred.

700 ᱇᱀᱀ *gyó ka-kyak*, seven hundred.

800 ᱈᱀᱀ *gyó ka-ku*, eight hundred.

900 ᱉᱀᱀ *gyó ka-kyót*, nine hundred.

999 ᱉᱉᱉ *gyó ka-kyót sa ka ka-kyót sa ka-kyót*, nine hundred and ninety-nine.

1000 ᱁᱀᱀᱀ *tong-hrók kát*, one thousand.

1010 ᱁᱀᱁᱀ *tong-hrók kát sa ka-ti*, one thousand and ten.

1011 ᱁᱀᱁᱁ *tong-hrók kát sa kát tháp*, one thousand and eleven.

1020 ᱁᱀᱂᱀ *tong-hrók kát sa ka nyat*, one thousand and twenty.

2000 ᱂᱀᱀᱀ *tong-hrók nyat*, two thousand.

10,000 ᱁᱀᱀᱀᱀ *hri-tsho kát*, ten thousand, one myriad.

búm tsho kát, or *búm kát*, one hundred thousand, one *lakh*.

so-yá kát, one million. *che-wó kát*, ten millions, one *kror*.

túng-chhúr kát, a hundred millions.

ther-búm kát, a thousand millions.

hrók hrik kát, a hundred thousand millions.

só só-yá kát, a billion.

The large numbers are taken from the Tibetan.

The Ordinals

are formed from the cardinals by affixing to the latter the particle *bo*; thus, *kát bo*, the first; *nyát bo*, the second; *sám bo*, the third; *fa-li bo*, the fourth, &c.

To this an adverbial signification may be given by adding *sa*, or *ká;* thus, *kát bo sa*, or *kát bo ká*, with reference to the first, firstly, or *lyáng*, may be prefixed, so, *lyáng kát bo ká*, in the first place, firstly.

Multiplicative terms,

expressing times, fold, are effected by affixing to the cardinal numbers *thyin*, or *dyóm;* or by prefixing *pho;* thus, *kát thyin*, *kát dyóm*, or *pho kát*, one time, once; *nyat thyin*, &c., twice; *sám dyóm*, &c., thrice; *pho fa-li*, four times, *pho fa-ngo bo re*, the fifth time, &c.

Distributive Numerals

may be formed by reduplicating the cardinals with *sa*, intervening; thus, *kát sa kát*, one by one, *nyat sa nyat*, two by two, &c.

Collective Numbers

are denoted, by different words, according to their significations; thus, the term to express two (persons or things), is expressed relatively (as shown under head of Pronouns), by affixing to the pronoun *nyi*, as, *hu-nyi*, those two persons or things; *nyum*, the two, both. Double (joined together) is rendered by *bryók*, &c., as *sa-dyar-mi bryók bo*, a double barrelled gun. Numbers, crowds, flocks, herds, &c., are expressed by *móng bo*, *zúm bo*, *á-dóp*, *á-nór*, &c.; thus, *mi-móng*, a crowd of people, *luk dóp*, a flock of sheep, *bik nór*, a herd of cows, &c.

A time, a turn, is expressed by *po-len*, (sometimes, *pho-len*); thus, *ka-su po-len gum*, it is my turn, &c., &c.

PART VI.

SYNTAX; FIGURATIVE AND HONORARY SPEECH; EXPLETIVES, &c., &c.

1.—*Of Syntax.*

The simplicity of the Lepcha language; the paucity of inflection, obviating the necessity of forms of concord in gender, number or case, or in the government of verbs, &c.; and with what has already, in this work, been said on the subject, leave little that needs explanation from syntax: a few remarks, however, may be deemed requisite.

In the formation of a sentence, the governing noun or the subject is, generally, placed first, the predicate follows; the object in the predicate clause precedes the verb; thus, *sa-kon kúng tyót*, Sakon felled a tree, (literally, Sakon tree felled).

The Article is seldom expressed, but when required the numeral adjective *kát*, one, *a;* or the particle *mu*, may be used; or, if definite, the particle *re*, (as explained under head of Articles, page 23); when employed they follow the noun; as, *cháng-gú kát*, a wolf.

Adjectives formed with the prefixed *á*, as a rule, follow the noun; thus, *cháng-gú á-tim*, a large wolf. Sometimes, however, the adjectives may precede the noun; thus, *á-má lóm*, a secret road; but this may be considered to be an hyperbaton, not the regular form.

When the article is employed with a noun in apposition, or with a noun and adjective, it follows the subsequent noun, or attribute; thus, *sa-kon ka-mór jem bo re*, Sakon the artist; *cháng-gú á-tim re*, the large wolf.

The objective case of a sentence, (either simple or compound), may be distinctly rendered by the inflected form of the article; thus, *cháng-gú á-tim re luk-kup á-chum rem thá,* the great wolf ate the small lamb, (lit. wolf great the, lamb small the, ate); *sa-thang nun sa-chi sa-gyeng sa-tyo sa-bur sa-ka sa-pyuk re re sa kát mum sót,* thar, choral, hog-deer, musk-deer, barking-deer, ibex, one of each was killed by a tiger, (lit. a tiger, *different animals,* of each, one killed). But in general, the articles are dispensed with altogether; they however become useful in indicating the objective case, in a sentence which might be ambiguous without inflection.

Adjectives commencing with *á,* when preceded by a noun, may sometimes drop the *á;* thus, *á-hrúm,* hot, *úng hrúm,* hot water; *á-hyang,* cold, *úng hyang,* cold water; *á-ham,* pure, unadulterated, *jer ham,* pure, unalloyed gold; *á-hyu,* plain, simple, without its adjunct, *zo hyu,* plain rice, without the husk, *ka-kyup hyu,* a plain ring, without its stone, &c.

But the retention or rejection of the *á,* is merely a matter of euphonic consideration, it is in general more elegantly retained; thus, *fa-lyeng á-náng,* a straightforward youth; *bu á-lim,* a heavy load; *chi á-chór,* sour beer, &c.

Nouns, when qualified by participial* or other verbal formatives, or by nouns connected with the relative participle *sa,* succeed their attributes; thus,

* It may have been perceived that in former occasions I have spelt the word participle in its form of an adjective the same as it is spelt when a noun; this occurred in the first instance by an error of the compositor's being overlooked: so, considering that one noun may be made to qualify another, also for uniformity's sake, I continued to have the word thus printed. In the present instance the adjective being somewhat separated from the noun, I have spelt it in its usual accepted way. It would, however, in my opinion, be better, if not more correct, to spell and pronounce it participal, the same as principal, (from princeps, particeps); adverbial might likewise be improved by being shortened to adverbal.

gát shang sa thám, a desirable thing; *dyák kung sa mi*, a blazing fire; *lók nón bo sa gi-chhó*, damaged goods; *shá-nye sa pa-hip*, a leaden pipe, &c.; (see, also, remarks on this subject, page 101).

Two nouns may be united together in the form of a relative possessive case, or, *in regimine;* in this form, the order of the words is the same as the English. When the affixed noun commences with *á*, the vowel is, invariably, dropped; thus, *á-ti*, an egg, *fo-ti*, a bird's egg, (instead of *fo sa á-ti*, the egg of a bird); *á-sháp*, a nest, *fo-sháp*, a bird's nest; *á-thu*, honey, *vót-thu*, *hu-thu*, *tung-bum-thu*, *sa-im-thu*, (different sorts of) bee's honey; *á-róng*, a horn, *bik-róng*, a cow's horn; *á-yu*, an eye (of needle, &c.), *ryum-yu*, a needle's eye; *á-thyák*, a head, *jat-thyák*, a pin's head; *á-rúk*, a young shoot, *po-rúk*, a bamboo shoot; *á-dót*, the remnant, the balance, *a-zóm dót*, the remains of food, &c.

But when ownership or possession is directly implied, the genitive case is more emphatic; it is also more dignified, and when significance is desired to be conveyed, this case would be, judiciously, used; should *á*, be the first letter of the succeeding noun, it would be correctly retained; thus, *lo-pan sa á-mik*, the eye of the master; *num-shim-nyo sa á-lut*, the heart of man; *sok sa á-sóm*, the spirit of life, &c.

Possessive pronouns precede the noun; when the latter commences with *á*, the vowel may, or may not be dropped; thus, *ka-su á-bo sa li, ká*, or, *ka-su bo sa li ká*, in the house of my father. The elliptical form, *ka-su á-bo li ká*, my father's house, is sometimes expressed, but this form, here, is slovenly, and rendering the sentence incomplete, it should not be acknowledged.

Some nouns, commencing with *á*, may bear elision when standing simply, but especially, when followed by some relative noun; thus, *á-ka*, the hand; *ka-jóm*, the fingers, *ka-tup*, the fist, *ka-dóm*, the thumb, &c. *á-thong*, the foot; *thong-jóm*, the toes, *thong-tung*, the heel, *thong pyól*, a foot print, &c. *á-thyák*, the head; *thyák-dám*, the crown of head, *thyák-ong*, the skull, *thyák-kám*, a pillow, &c. *á-dyáng*, the leg; *dyáng-lyók*, the sole of foot, *dyáng pók*, to kick forwards, *dyáng gór ayók*, to kick backwards, &c. *á-mik*, the eye; *mik-chóm*, the eye-lash, *mik-myóng*, the eye-brow, *mik-grúng*, a tear, &c.; *á-fo*, a tooth, *fo-nyel*, the gums, *fo-góm*, the molar teeth, *fo-zal*, the incisors, *fo-bík*, the eye-tooth, a tusk, &c. *á-tsóm*, the hair, *tsóm bleng*, a single haïr, *tsóm-rík*, a pig-tail, *tsóm-chong*, a hair-knot, &c., &c.

Postpositions, commencing with *á*, may, likewise, when affixed to a noun, often drop the vowel, whereby the sense may in a degree become modified; thus, or, *li sa á-plang*, or, *li á-plang*, upon the house, *li-plang ká*, on the house-top; *on á-plang*, upon the horse, *hu on-plang thúl*, he rode on horseback. *á-pún*, the side of, *gyám-tsho-pún, úng-kyong-pún, sa lóm-pún ká*, on the sea-shore, the river-bank, and road-side.

Other prefixed particles, besides *á*, are sometimes dropped, but chiefly when in conjunction with a following word, forming a compound term; thus, *sa-tsuk*, the sun; *tsuk-kyar*, the west, *tsuk-náng*, the meridian, *tsuk-tsur*, a sun-beam, &c. *ta-só*, yesterday, *só só*, lately, *só ren thyák bo*, an acquaintance of yesterday, &c. *sa-nyim*, the day, *nyim-phyet*, mid-day, *nyim rel la sa ayok*, daily work; *so-náp*, the night, *náp-mo*, the evening, *náp pa lúk ka*, evening and morning, &c.

A word may, sometimes, assume a prefixed syllable without any change in the part of speech; thus, *ayo*, or, *sa-ayo*, before, formerly, (time); *hán*, or, *na-hán*, before, prior, antecedent, (time or space), &c.

Some prefixed syllables bear a legitimate degree of change; thus, *pa-zók*, *pun-zók*, *puk-zók*, jungle; *pa-nyóm*, *pun-nyóm*, *put-nyóm*, an old man; *so-mat*, (lit. the state of the weather), altered to *sung-mat*, (commonly, but not so correctly spelt *sung-mut*), the wind, &c., &c.; (see, also, under head of commutable prefixed syllables, page 20).

Different local pronunciations, however, and often ignorance, &c., render the change, in the first syllables of dissyllabic words, very common, and, sometimes, very irregular; this disorganizing tendency should be, altogether, discouraged; and the proper prefixed syllable of each word, when decided on, should be adhered to. This principle should be laid down as a canon, and systematically impressed on the Lepchas.

In the use of the Plural signs, when the noun is indefinite, the sign is affixed; thus, *ma-ró sang li*, the people spoke. But when the number is defined, the sign is unnecessary; thus, *bík fa-li mák*, four cows died.

Where the plural may be inferred, through the aid of any connecting clause, a single sign may be sufficient to pluralize several nouns; thus, *fyan nun, li, nyót, sa shing pang tyup fát*; or by summing all to a climax, the sign may be dispensed with; thus, * * * * * * * * * * *shing, lyáng tyang, tyup fát*, the enemy laid waste the houses, fields and gardens; or, the houses, fields, and gardens, the whole country was laid waste by the enemy.

But where no inferential word or clause exists, it is better to attach the sign to each noun; thus, *li pang, shi pang, sa shing pang dop nón*, the houses, household goods, and gardens were burned.

When a noun, in the plural, is qualified by an adjective, the plural sign may succeed, or precede the adjective; thus, ᰕᰛᰩ ᰣᰛᰤᰫᰮ ᰠᰵ, or, ᰕᰛᰩ ᰠᰵ ᰣᰛᰤᰫᰮ *ma-ró á-ryúm sang*, or, *ma-ró sang á-ryúm*, good people. The former is, perhaps, the more idiomatic.

Pronominal adjectives, generally, precede the noun; thus, ᰣᰛᰬ ᰇᰨ *á-re chho*, this book; ᰠᰛᰬ ᰕᰛᰩ *sa-re ma-ró*, which man? or, any man, &c.

The Postpositive Particles ᰃᰨᰛᰫᰵ *go-rúng*, ᰃᰵ ᰜ *gang la*, and ᰜ *la*, may be separated from the Pronoun or Adverb by a word, or clause; thus, ᰊᰨ ᰃᰨᰛᰫᰵ *to go-rúng*, whosoever; ᰊᰨ ᰕᰛᰩ ᰃᰨᰛᰫᰵ *to ma-ró go-rúng*, what person, soever, ᰊᰨ ᰉᰧᰴ ᰃᰨᰛᰫᰵ *to nyi go-rúng*, whosoever there may be. ᰠᰛᰬ ᰃᰵ ᰜ *sa-re gang la*, whichsoever, ᰠᰛᰬ ᰃᰦᰳ ᰃᰵ ᰜ, ᰜᰤ *sa-re gát gang la, lya*, whichsoever you please, take. ᰊᰨ ᰃᰵ ᰜ *to gang la*; whosoever; ᰃᰨ ᰊᰨ ᰠ ᰣᰀᰪᰱ ᰃᰨ ᰃᰵ ᰜ, ᰝᰩ ᰠ ᰡᰫ ᰂᰩᰭ ᰉᰧᰴ ᰢᰪᰵ ᰣ *go to sa á-kup go gang la, hó sa shú khók nyi wung a*, whosesoever child I may be, what business is it of yours. ᰡᰫ ᰜ *shú la*, whatever, whatsoever, every; ᰡᰫ ᰜ ᰕ ᰉᰧᰴ ᰍᰬ *shú la ma nyin ne*, nothing, ᰂᰨ ᰉᰧᰴ *kho nyi*, it is of use, ᰡᰫ ᰂᰨ ᰜ ᰕ ᰉᰧᰴ ᰍᰬ *shú kho la ma nyin ne*, it is of no use, ᰡᰫ ᰋᰤᰨ ᰜ ᰕ ᰂᰪᰰ ᰍᰬ *shú thyo la ma khun ne*, I can hear nothing. ᰊᰨ ᰜ *to la*, every one; ᰊᰨ ᰕᰛᰩ ᰀᰦᰳ ᰜ ᰕ ᰓᰦᰮ ᰍᰬ *to ma-ró kát la ma bám ne*, there is not one single person remaining.

Dissyllabic verbs, compounded of two words, may be separated by a qualifying word; thus, ᰌᰬᰰ ᰛᰧᰴ *den-ri*, to believe, ᰌᰬᰰ ᰀᰦᰮ ᰛᰧᰴ *den kám ri*, to have little faith, ᰣᰬ ᰌᰬᰰ ᰀᰦᰮ ᰛᰧᰴ ᰓᰨ ᰠᰵ ᰅᰦ *e den kám ri bo sang ngá*, O ye of little faith; ᰀᰤᰩᰰ ᰌᰤᰭ *kyón-dyak*, to pity, to feel compassion, ᰀᰤᰩᰰ ᰍᰮᰴ ᰌᰤᰭ *kyón nam dyak*, to have exceeding compassion, (see, also, the same construction in the negative form, page 109).

But this disseverance does not take place where the word is a substantive; thus, *kyón-dit*, compassion, pity; *kyón-dit á-tim*, great pity; *tuk-nóm*, a nose, *tuk-nóm kung-kóng bo*, an acquiline nose, &c.

Pronominal adjectives and adverbs, when expressed relatively, may, abbreviated, be repeated emphatically after the verb; thus, *hó sa-lem nóng lem go la nóng sho*, whither you go, thither will I go also; *hó sa-bi bám bi go la bám sho*, wheresoever you dwell, I shall also dwell; *hó sa-thá mák thá go la mák sho*, whenever you die, I shall die also; *hu sa-lo zúk lo, go la zúk sho*, as he does, so shall I do; *hu sa-tet zúk tet go la zúk sho*, I will do as much as he does; *á-yú sa-re ching re, sa-re gát re thop sho*, whatever you think, whatever you desire, you shall obtain, &c.

The preceding adverb may be omitted, and the succeeding verb and adverb may, then, be expressed as a compound noun; thus, *go hu nóng lem nóng sho*, I will go where he goes, I will go his whither-ward.

In speaking of the 1*st*, 2*nd* and 3*rd* persons, singly, the singular number (not as in some languages, the plural) is always employed; thus, or, *go á-dom*, or, *hó mum li*, I spoke to *thee*; *hó nun hum byi*, *thou* gavest him, &c; (not even in honorary language does this form ever change).

The instrumental case, when the noun governs an active verb, may, generally, be used instead of the Nominative; thus, or, *hu li*, or, *hu nun li*, he said. But it cannot be, correctly, used in connection with an intransitive verb; thus, *hu dang*, (not, *hu nun dang*), he ran. It may often be, advantageously, employed in indicating the governing noun, especially in a compound sentence, where the word may happen to be far separated from the governed verb. It is also, sometimes, made serviceable as an intervention between two symphonous letters; thus, *hu nun hum byi*, (instead of, *hu hum byi*), he gave him.

Words, capable of direct inflection, (as pronouns), may be inflected, when governed by transitive verbs; thus, *go á-yúm li*, I told you, or, I spoke to you.

Verbs signifying –sending and conveying– when governing nouns, referring to a second person, require the aid of a postposition; thus, (or, or, *go nun hu ká*, (or, *hu lyáng*, or, *hu lyáng ká)*, *yuk byat*, I sent a letter to him, (not, him a letter); *go hu ka ká yuk rem klóng*, I sent the letter by his hands, or, in his charge, (not him with the letter), &c.; *ka-su lyáng bu-di*, bring it to me, &c.

The Substantive verbs *go*, *gó*, *&c.*, do not inflect a noun; thus, *go hu gum*, I am he; *hu ma-ró re* (not, *rem) gum*, *to nun á-dyut ká gye fát*, he is the man who conquered in battle.

In the Imperative mood, the verb *kón*, inflects the noun; thus, *ka-sum nón kón*, let me go; not so in the Hortative mood, which is expressed by means of the particle *ká;* thus, *ka-yú nóng ká*, let we (not us) go.

Nouns are not inflected, by simple postpositions, (as in English they, generally, are by prepositions); thus, *hó sa*, of thee, (lit. of thou); *hu tun-dók ká*, on his account, (lit. on account of he); *go hu kón óp*, I fired towards him (he). &c.

In referring to a subject, said, thought or done, &c., as usual the noun or pronoun, in general, comes first; the verb, preceded by a relative adverb, the last; thus, ***hu nun, hu-yú ká, ka-su á-mlem ik sa-thá la ma shi na sho, yang li.*** he said unto them, you shall never see my face again (lit. he uuto them, ******, thus said);

[Lepcha text] *tá-pan ká, on bu-di, yang dun na,* tell the groom to bring the horse, (lit. to the groom, the horse bring, thus tell); [Lepcha text] *go nun hum, no o, yo li,* I told him to go, (lit. I to him, go, thus said); [Lepcha text] *go, á-re nyák ka um pá, yang ching ma,* I thought that this was very nice, (lit. I, this very nice is, thus thought).

Causive Conjunctions are, generally, affixed to the verb; thus, [Lepcha text] (or, [Lepcha text]), [Lepcha text] *ma-ró hláp bo nyi nun mát bá,* (or, *nun mát ren*), *kum-yam bo gum,* the man is clever, because he is learned. Illative conjunctions are, usually, detached; thus, [Lepcha text] *ma-ró hláp bo nyi, á'r nun mát lung hu kum-yam bo gum,* the man is learned, therefore he is clever.

In the following sentence, I give examples of some conjunctions and adverbs, by which it may be seen how they may be employed. They may be distinguished in the transliteration, by being printed in Roman type, and in the translation, by being printed in Italics. [Lepcha text] *hu mák* nun mát bán, *go sák-dak gum,* yáng na á-lo do *ryú* pú, a'r nun mát bá yo ma go na gang, *hu na zú* gang, *hu-do sa ma-zu* sa *á-lut ká á-duk zak bo* ka-tá zón *ma go na re,* shen la *hu sa num-nu sang gun na ká fram lyáng nyi túng,* yang *shú* go-thom la *ma nyin ne.* I am sorry *that* he is dead, *but, perhaps,* it is better *as it is, for if it were otherwise, had* he still lived, there can be *no doubt, that not only* he would have been afflicted in body *and* mind, *but* would have been a source of anxiety to all his friends.

The peculiarity, in the verb – to give – represented by [Lepcha text] *bo,* and [Lepcha text] *byi,* not having been noticed before, may be here shown. The former is used, when governing the 1st and 2nd persons; the latter, when governing the 3rd person; thus, *ka-sum bo*, give me; *á-dom bo*, give thee; *hum byi*, give him; *ka-yúm bó*, give us; *á-yúm bo*, give ye; *hu-yúm byi*, give them. It is the same, if the verb be used in a transitive sense; thus, *ka-sum li bo*, speak to me; *hum dun byi*, tell him.

In speech the future particle *sho*, like the future sign in English, is generally abbreviated; thus, *go nóng sho*, would be pronounced *go nóng sh'*, I'll go; so, *hu di sh'*, he 'll come; *hó mát sh'*, thou 'lt do it, &c.

Neither prescribed time nor space will admit a particularizing of every little point that may occur in the formation and construction of sentences, enough, however, has been said to facilitate the learner in acquiring the language, and this is the object of this work. I shall conclude this subject, by showing an example of the diversity of significations, which a single word may possess, and the influence these exert in modifying expressions of speech.

Though the language abounds in synonyms, yet numerous words bear many various meanings, both simple and in combination with other words, effecting great play and power of speech. I shall take, as an example, the word *mát*, giving some of its significations.

mát, to do, to make, &c. 2, to become, to acquire; *chho ma mát na gang, muk-nyám lyáng mán-pó, vón lyáng ma nyin ne*, unless you become holy, except to the land of departed spirits (hades), to no other place shall you go, (*Ta-she sung,* Tashe's history). 3, to effect; *hu pa-no mát bám*, he affects, assumes the king. 4, to suppose; *á-re li rem mát ta*, suppose, imagine, assume, (make out) this to be the house. 5, to befall; *hu ká sa-thi zak*, misfortune has befallen him. 6, to make a custom, habit of; *hu ngól lúk mát*, he is in the habit of rising early. 7, used as a substantive, for the thing, or, action; *hu á-lang kát mát li, á-nye kát mát li,* he now says one thing, presently another.

8, except, only; *á-thól mát ma nóng ne,* I shall go, only, a short distance, (lit. except near, I shall not go). 9, till, until; *hu ta-só mát ma thi ne,* he did not arrive till yesterday. 10, including, along with, in addition to; *kóm mo sa á-kup mát,* including the capital, and interest; *kóm sa dum mát byi,* to give clothes, as well as money. 11, when affixed to substantives, it transmutes the sense to a verb; thus, *ayok,* work, *ayok mát,* to work; also sometimes expresses, *emphatically,* to do, or, effect; thus, *á-mik,* the eye, *mik mát,* to spy, to pry into; *gang la á-yáng la ma mát ne,* but it was, indeed, of no effect, answered no purpose; the sense is also sometimes modified; thus, *á-kup,* a child, *kup mát lóng,* to *adopt,* and bring up a child; *lóm sa mát,* to make preparations for the road; *á-mlem mát,* to make a face, to be sulky, sullen, &c: (see also its agency in forming a causal, page 93). 12, implies also, to have sexual intercourse, (*ta-ayu mát*); *mát zang,* an assistant, an abettor; also a concubine. 13, preceded by *shang,* intention is inferred; thus, *go nóng shang mát, yáng á-lang ma nóng na sho,* I intended to go, but I shall not go now. 14, when preceded by *zang,* it signifies pretence; thus, *ma shi na zang mát,* to pretend not to see. 15, succeeded by *bá, bán, lung,* or *ren,* gives signification of, through, by means of, on account of, &c; so, *zo chhú sa mát lung,* provisions for (on account of) the road, (see pages, 84 and 87). 16, *mát-bá,* preceded by *sa,* implies comparison; thus, *hlo sa mát bá, li á-chum gum,* compared with the hill, the house is small. 17, followed by *gang,* forms a conditional; thus, *hó ka-sum bo mát gang, go á-dom ma ki na sho,* If, or, provided you give it to me I shall not prosecute you. 18, followed by *lóm*, it expresses conduct; so, *hu sa mát-lóm á-zuk gum,* his conduct is excellent. 19, with *lu*, affixed, it signifies, mode of doing anything, fashion, rule; so, *mát-lu dok la mát,* to act according to fashion. 20, with the plural sign affixed, a substantive is formed; thus, *mát pang,* actions, *mát pang sa á-pót ma thop ne,* not to receive the fruits of one's labour. With the participle, present and future, (Gerund), it also expresses nouns; thus, *hu mát tung á-tĩm zúk,* he performed a great deed, *á-lang ren, á-do mát shang, ryú la nyi ma o,* from the present time let your deeds be good. 21, with *shang ká,* affixed, it may refer to a period of time; thus, *go sa-ayák sám mát shang ká zúk lel sho,* in the space of three days, (lit. in the work of three days), I shall finish it. 22, with *shang,* and the article *re,* affixed, it may be rendered emphatic and special, – what ought to be done, – so, *mát shang re chho gum,* the necessary thing, is religion. 23, with *la,* affixed, it acts as an adverbial medium between the verb and its subject or qualification; thus, *ryú la mát la zúk,* do it well, (after a goodly fashion); it also acts the part of a postposition, (or, English preposition); as, *tsuk-kyar mát la ngak,* look *towards* the west, &c.

2.—*Of Figurative language.*

What, in Lepcha, may be considered a distinct part of the language, is, *tung-bór,* (or, *thám-bór*), lit. a hint, an innuendo; therefore, *tung-bór ring,* may be called, a figurative language. It is formed of words, to which a figurative, or metaphorical meaning is attached; thus, *mik chám,* to close the eyes, hence, to die; *klót,* to be stiff, = to die, *klót bo,* a stiff 'un, &c. In this language, the Lepchas are fond of speaking, constantly interspersing their colloquy with it;

hence, it is necessary for the person desirous of being conversant with the Lepcha language to acquaint himself with this mode of speech; not only to the end, that he may attain a thorough knowledge of the tongue; but, also, to save himself from the imputation of being considered dull of comprehension; for as the Lepchas say, *ma-ró yam bo nun, bong kyang tyu ren, mik kyang tyu ren shi wung, ya sho,* a man of wit will understand, by seeing the corner of the mouth move, or the corner of the eye twinkle.

The following are some examples of words,

English.	*Ordinary words.*	*Tung-bór.*
Water,	*úng,*	*tur-jám mo.*
Fire,	*mi,*	*tung-yal mo.*
Rice,	*zo,*	*tur-fám mo.*
Do. boiled,	*zo men,*	*num-or mo.*
Milk,	*nyen,*	*túng tshóng.*
Meat,	*man,*	*má-ri.*
Spirit (liquor),	*chi,*	*num-fyeng mo.*
Fish,	*ngo,*	*pun-shal mo.*
Dog,	*ka-jú,*	*shim húl bo.*
Cow,	*bik,*	*ta-lóm mo.*
Pig,	*món,*	*num-júr mo.*
Goat,	*sa-ár,*	*bong gyáp bo.*
A cock,	*hik bu,*	*lum bu.*
Rat,	*ka-lók,*	*bong jak bo.*
A bear,	*sa-mo,*	*tung-gop mo.*

English.	*Ordinary words.*	*Tung-bór.*
Monkey,	*sa-hu,*	*mlem ryúm bo.*
Woman,	*ta-ayu,*	*num-lóp mo.*
A Lepcha,	*róng,*	*mo-tun-chi.*
A Hindoo,	*lúm,*	*king zang bo.*
A priest,	*yúk-mun,*	*thám hyir bo.*
An orphan,	*ryót kup,*	*ta-gól tuk-dim.*
A rupee,	*kóm kát,*	*zer bo.*
An eight áná piece,	*thá-lá kát,*	*num-bóng lóp.*
A road,	*lóm.*	*ta-mo.*
A tree,	*kúng,*	*sa-shim.*
Fire wood,	*sháng,*	*num-ngál mo.*
A large basket,	*tung-gryóng,*	*sa-ót.*
A net,	*sung-li,*	*ka-chór.*
To bite,	*tsúk,*	*rán.*
To be born,	*gyek,*	*klyák.*
Day to break,	*so-sóng ngún,*	*tur-zut lún.*
Stolen goods,	*tuk-mo sa thám,*	*num-shal mo.*
The house is burned,	*li dop nón,*	*bám túr nón.*
To part with,	*thám lyót,*	*vyal nyón.*

hó dor-je-ling ka pur-gyeng bi zo nyón sho, you will have to eat lentils (Ervum lens) in Dorjeling; means, you will be put into jail, if you go to Dorjeling.

&c. &c.

3.—*Of Honorific Language.*

Honorific, or respectful language (*she-so ring*), may also be considered a distinct part of the Lepcha tongue. It is used by inferiors to superiors; likewise, among equals, when a polite and courteous mode of speech is desired to be employed. It may be called the court language; most of the words are derived from the Tibetan, as may be seen by the following examples.

English,	*Ordinary,*	*Honorary words.*
To walk, to go,	*lóm, nóng,*	*chan.*
To sit,	*ngán,*	*jú.*
To rise,	*lúk,*	*jóng.*
To look, to see,	*shi,*	*zu.*
To speak,	*li,*	*súng.*
To hear, to listen,	*nyan,*	*sán.*
To accept, to eat,	*lya, zo,*	*je.*
To give, to grant,	*bo, byi,*	*nóng.*
To forget,	*myón,*	*yel.*
To remember,	*sák nón,*	*kú kre bo sun.*
To know,	*ya,*	*khyen.*
Body,	*ma-zu,*	*kú.*
Head,	*á-thyák,*	*ú.*
Hair of ditto,	*á-tsóm,*	*ú-kró.*
Head dress,	*tuk-tuk,*	*ú-shó.*
Turban,	*pók,*	*ú-thong.*
Pillow,	*thyák-kám,*	*ú-nge.*
Mouth,	*á-bong,*	*she.*

English,	*Ordinary,*	*Honorary words.*
Face,	*á-mlem*	*she-dong.*
Mustachios,	*bong-mat,*	*she-gyan.*
Beard, (Hair of face, &c),	*ka-yat,*	*she-gyan.*
Lips,	*á-dúl,*	*she-pá.*
Spittle,	*dyúk,*	*she-chhóp.*
Blood,	*vi,*	*ku-tshál.*
Tongue,	*á-li,*	*ják.*
Tooth,	*á-fo,*	*tshem.*
Eye,	*á-mik,*	*chan.*
Eye-lash,	*mik-chóm,*	*chan-shok.*
Eye-brow,	*mik-myóng*	*chan-kró*
Tears,	*mik-grúng,*	*chan-chhóp.*
Nose,	*tuk-nóm,*	*sháng.*
Ear,	*á-nyor,*	*nyan.*
Hand,	*á-ka,*	*chhók.*
Finger,	*ka-jóm,*	*chhók-sor.*
Foot,	*á-thong,*	*shóp.*
Heel,	*thong-tung,*	*shóp-ting.*
Belly,	*ta-bak,*	*kú-to.*
Clothes,	*dum,*	*na-zó.*
To weep,	*hryóp,*	*shúm.*
To be angry,	*sák lyák,*	*gong-hre.*
In the presence of,	*dun ká,*	*kúm dun.*

English,	*Ordinary,*	*Honorary words.*
To enter presence,	*dun ká vón,*	*kúm dun chó.*
Father,	*á-bo,*	*yáp.*
Mother,	*á-mo,*	*yám.*
To be born,	*gyek,*	*tóm nón.*
A son,	*á-kup,*	*se.*
A name,	*á-bryáng,*	*tshán.*
A letter,	*yuk,*	*chá-rí.*
A handkerchief,	*ta-ró,*	*chhók-pí.*
Water,	*úng,*	*chhóp.*
Food,	*á-zóm,*	*sa.*
To serve up ditto,	*á-zóm so,*	*sa phu.*
To wash,	*chóng,*	*su.*
To be weary,	*pyal,*	*nyil.*
A dream,	*móng,*	*nál-lóm.*
To recline, to rest,	*dyór dá,*	*nól.*
To sleep,	*mik-kráp,*	*zum.*
To be sick,	*dak,*	*nyung.*
To grow old,	*gán nóng,*	*kú-kre.*
To die,	*mák,*	*krong.*
A corpse,	*á-fung,*	*púr.*
To burn ditto,	*á-fung fan,*	*púr jú.*
To bury ditto,	*fung lap,*	*púr tek.*
A sepulchre, a tomb,	*chók,*	*kú-góng*
	&c.	&c.

Letters and despatches always commence with, and are, generally, continued in a complimentary strain; thus, *gun na khyen nung sa zu wung sa pa-no krọ́k bo ká, vyet kup, ka-bum mát lung, yang shu,* to the great king, the omniscient and all-seeing, his humble slave, with folded hands, thus prefers his address, &c.

4.—*Of Expletives,*— *tshuk-pryóm.*

Numerous words in the Lepcha language are found, to each of which a second word is attached, the latter often bearing no apparent relative meaning. Some of these may take their derivation from words in other tongues, or, like words in *Tung-bór ring,* may have lost the peculiar signification they may once have possessed. A few admit of a degree of disconnection; thus, *mát shóp,* to do, to act, *mát pang shóp pang,* deeds, actions, &c; and some do bear a correlative meaning; as, *sa-tsuk sa-mik,* (the latter formed from *á-mik,* the eye, = most precious), the sun — the most glorious orb. Many however undoubtedly have no distinct signification, corresponding to their preceding words, and may be regarded as mere expletives. The following are examples, of words and their expletives.

English,	*Substantive words,*	*Expletives.*
The world,	*suk-dum,*	*lung-ming.*
Stars,	*sa-hór,*	*pur-du.*
Water,	*úng,*	*vyóng.*
Earth,	*fat,*	*let.*
Blood,	*vi,*	*nyo.*
Meat,	*man,*	*kit.*
Flesh,	*á-chók,*	*á-byit.*

English,	*Substantives words,*	*Expletives.*
Vegetables,	*bi,*	*dong.*
Weeds (rubbish),	*múk,*	*shók.*
Cloth,	*dum,*	*dang.*
Wood,	*kúng,*	*lang.*
Iron,	*pun-jeng,*	*pun-lang.*
An evil spirit,	*múng,*	*má.*
A song,	*vam,*	*dum.*
A drum,	*tung-dár,*	*lung-ming.*
A year (time),	*nám,*	*túm.*
Hastily,	*sung-shang,*	*tun-dón.*
An article,	*mlo,*	*blang.*
A tooth,	*á-fo,*	*á-ki.*
A bird,	*fo,*	*yu.*
A monkey,	*sa-hu,*	*pa-lap.*
Love (joy),	*á-gó,*	*á-nyi.*
Head,	*á-thyák,*	*á-lo.*
Prudent, thriftly,	*ka-tsám,*	*ka-ji.*
A defeat,	*á-flyek,*	*á-hlám.*
Oppression,	*án-zo,*	*án-di.*
Breath,	*á-sóm,*	*á-bum.*
A door,	*vyeng,*	*grong.*
Ease, quietness,	*á-kyat,*	*á-dyáng.*
To cherish,	*dak,*	*nyit.*

5.—*Of the call to Animals; and Infantine language.*

The Lepchas have special terms for calling all descriptions of domestic animals; and the words used when addressing infants form, in themselves, quite a little dialect. I shall not weary the learner with a detail of the above, but it behooves him, who would master the Lepcha language, to make himself conversant in this parlance; otherwise he may incur the displeasure of the husbandman, and be disdainfully told, *hó thám-chang ma ma ya ne*, you do not know how to call animals! or the indignant mother may reprehensively exclaim, *hó ayeng-bóng ring ma thyák ne*, you are not acquainted with infantile speech! The terms may be found in their respective places in the Lepcha Dictionary.

6.—*Of Prosody.*

The Monosyllabic form of the Lepcha language renders the pronunciation very easy. The Lepchas are remarkably uniform in the pronunciation of words, and to this we must look to obtain correct spelling. The orthography is governed by the orthoepy.

In the pronunciation of dissyllables, whether the word be simple or compound, the accent, as a rule, falls on the last syllable; thus, *sa-ryóm*, an otter; *num-vóm*, united in the wedlock, married; *ka-jak*, the fore-finger; *tan to*, to know by experience, *tá-chók*, a whip, *to-dat*, equality, uniformity, *mú-tik*, a pearl, &c.

In words compounded of the particle *bo*, and other suffixes, the accent necessarily rests on the first syllable, the substantive part of the word; thus, *mi-bo*, a trance, *mát lu shóp lu*, modes, fashions, &c., *to-mo*, trousers, *lóm bo*, a walker, &c.

In an interrogative sentence the voice (as in English, &c.,) rises on the final accentuation; thus, *sa-ba nóng shang a*, where are you going to? *shú ka te*, what is it?

The Lepchas have no books written in verse. When reading prose they are fond of reciting the subject in measured cadence, and the wandering Bards (their priests), chaunt their tales and legends in sonorous and rhythmic strains. They have numerous songs, but many are hardly intelligible, being chiefly composed of *tung-bór*, the inference of which has been lost, and of expletives to complete the numbers. The numbers run smoothly, in general from five to ten measures; they, however, are not always regularly sustained; the verse is mostly iambic. The following is a specimen of the commencement of one of their songs—

˘ ¯ | ˘ ¯ | ˘ ¯ | ˘ ¯
sa-mi | *tung-gum* | *á-nóm* | *sang nyá,*
sa-mur | *nyo bu* | *chhet nón* | *ne a.*

which may be paraphrased;

From behind the fire, sisters dear,
The flood has ceased to pour good cheer.

An allusion to the female cup-bearers, sitting behind the fire-hearth, to whom the Bacchanalians are calling for more "good cheer." *mur-nyo bu*, is in mythology, the serpent that led the waters from *ta-lya da*, the profundity of waters in *tang-dek*, the regions under the earth; hence, running streams; (in contradistinction to *mur-nyo bóng*, still, standing waters, lakes). The mythology is romantic in the extreme, and full of interest; it has its abode in dream-land, and teems with spirits good and evil, with fays and fairies, wraiths and goblins. But since the Tibetans forced on them their barbarous Buddhist creed, and especially since the influx of Europeans, and natives of the plains of India, they have become contaminated; the Lepchas are losing all their simplicity and liveliness of fancy, their innocent and attractive idealism, their artless, guileless character are fast dying out, and being replaced by that which has been taught them,—duplicity, calculating selfishness, and all that is vile and evil.

7.—*Of Division of time.*

The Lepchas apportion the day into periods regulated by the rise and decline of the sun; thus, *so-sóng*, day-break; *sa-tsuk tsár*, the first rays of the sun, sun-rise; *sa-tsuk chi li*, when the sun has fully risen; to *sa-tsuk zán li*, when the sun is in full power; to *sa-tsuk náng*, when the sun is in the zenith, meridian, noon; after which *sa-tsuk gye li*, when the sun commences its declination, afternoon, to about the end of the third quarter; when *sa-tsuk yo li*, begins and continues; till *sa-tsuk that*, sun-set; after which *náp-mo*, the evening sets in.

sa-ayák, is a day of 24 hours; including *sa-nyi*, the day and *so-náp*, the night.

dun-hrók, is a period of seven days, (derived from the Tibetan བདུན་ཕྲག *bdun-phrag*, a week, a se'n-night. The following are the Lepcha days of the week; *mi sa-ayák*, Sunday; *úng sa-ayák*, Monday; *lang sa-ayák*, Tuesday; *nyen sa-ayák*, Wednesday; *sung-mat sa-ayák*, Thursday; *fat sa-ayák*, Friday; *pun-jeng sa-ayák*, Saturday. But these are seldom employed now, and in fact are becoming obsolete; the Tibetan terms are almost invariably made use of, these take their names from the planets (གཟའ *gzah*, a planet; including the sun and moon); thus, གཟའ་བདུན *gzah-bdun*, the seven planets.

zá nyi-má, (the Sun) Sunday.

zá dá-wá, (the Moon), Monday.

zá mik-má, (Mars), Tuesday.

zá hlák-bo, (Mercury), Wednesday.

zá phúr-bo, (Jupiter), Thursday.

zá pá-sáng (Venus), Friday.

zá phem-bo, (Saturn), Saturday.

The months are calculated by moons, of which they allot the usual twelve to the year. The month or moon is called *la-vo*, but the name of a month, as a period, is *nyóm*. The following are the order and names of the months; *ayit nyóm*, *rá nyóm*, *már nyóm*, *kur-nyit nyóm*, *kur-sóng nyóm*, *thón-nyóm*, *sam nyóm*, *num-tsám nyóm*, *blúng nyóm*, *num-kum nyóm*, *pur-vim nyóm*, *glú nyóm*.

nám, is a year, in Lepcha. The new year (*nám-bu*), varies according to the date of the new moon, and according as the period is altered by the addition of an intercallary month (*la-vo sho*, or *la-vo nyet*), which is added about once in three years to regulate the lunar with the solar time.

Long periods are computed by cycles of 12 years (*nám kor*, or *lo kor* [ལོ་སྐོར་], lit. a cycle of years), the following are the names and order; 1, *ka-lók nám* the rat year. 2, *lóng nám*, the ox year. 3, *sa-thang nám*, the tiger year. 4, *kum-thyóng nám*, the eagle year. 5, *sa-dyar nám*, the thunder-bolt year. 6, *bu nám*, the serpent year. 7, *on nám*, the horse year. 8, *luk nám*, the sheep year. 9, *sa-hu nám*, the ape year. 10, *hik nám*, the fowl year. 11, *ka-jú nám*, the dog year. 12, *món nám*, the hog year.

8.—*Colloquial Sentences.*

How are you; how is your health?	*hó sa-lo gó, ma-zu zóng bám a.*
What is your name?	*á-do á-bryáng sa-lo gó.*
What are you doing?	*hó shú-mát tung gó.*

Where are you going?	*hó sa-bá nóng ngung a.*
Where do you wish to go?	*hó sa-bá nóng gát shang a.*
Where is your home?	*á-do bám lyáng sa-bi nyi wung a.*
Is it far or near?	*ma-rum á-thól a.*
When do you return?	*sa-thá lót nóng shang a.*
Give my compliments to your father?	*á-bo ká khám-ri mát.*
What business is he employed in?	*hu shú gen bu wung a.*
Are the crops flourishing?	*nyót thok tar rung a.*
There is not likely to be a plentiful harvest.	*thok pa-ba la ma go na pú.*
Why do you think so?	*hó shú-mát á-lom ching ngung gó.*
It seems as if it would be so.	*á-lom ngún shang ka pú lyok.*
There has been little rain this year.	*nám so-myáng mán nyi*
How far is it from Dorjeling to Tibet, viâ Sikim.	*dor-je-ling nun pat ká, ren-jong sa lóm nun, sa-tet ru a.*
You are hungry, have something to eat and drink.	*hó krit-dak gum, á-zóm á-than sa-re lya.*
No thank you, (it is your graciousness), I am not hungry; I have no appetite.	*mán, thú-je chhi, go krit ma dak ne, táng-kó ma lú ne.*

Drink some beer.	*chi thang le.*
It does not agree with me.	*hu ka-sum thát sho.*
Plain water and food alone agree with me.	*úng zo ka-tá zón ka-sum jit sho.*
Select whatever you like.	*hó sa-re gát re tham ma.*
Cook the food.	*á-zóm zúk.*
Boil the soup, boil the meat, and roast the fowl.	*tuk-tak ka, man ngo, sa hik il.*
Make a meat stew.	*man sa á-chóm zúk.*
Toast the bread and infuse the tea.	*khú i, sa chó pot.*
Bake the bread and bake the potatoes in the ashes, also the arums in ditto.	*khú su, búk byúp, sa sung-kri ayúr.*
Eat slowly, do not gobble your food.	*sa-gang zo, á-zóm ma fam mun.*
Do not stuff your mouth with food.	*á-zóm ma móp pun.*
Do not smoke, snuff, or chew tobacco; they are filthy and injurious habits.	*tóm-ku ma-thang ma fóm mun, sa phi-ling ma thang ngun, nyóm mung sa mu lók kung sa lóng-sho gum.*
Wash your face.	*á-do á-mlem flet.*
Give me my shirt, coat, waistcoat, trowsers, socks, and shoes.	*ka-su pa-hók, ko, ta-li, tó-mo thong-shuk, hlóm bo o.*

Where is my comb and brush, I wish to comb my hair? — *hrit sa pak-zu sa-bá nyi wung a, go á-tsóm krat gát.*

I am going out, be so good as to give me my hat, gloves, and stick. — *go lyáng nóng sho, ka-su tuk-tuk, ka-shuk, sa pa-túng bo le.*

Bring that box, bundle, and umbrella. — *o-re rom, bat, sa dú bu-di.*

Open and re-close the umbrella. — *dú ráng sa lót hyup.*

What is the price of this, at what do you value it? — *á-re á-fár sa-tet, hó sa-tet gong ngung gó.*

It is very dear. — *á-gyáp kú gum.* [bám.

I think it cheap. — *go, ke ma, yang ching*

It is not worth as much, I would not estimate it so high. — *o-tet ma wa ne, go o-tet ma ri ne.*

I spoke hyperbolically, without thinking. — *go ma ching na mát, kyam-hyat mát lung li.*

What is the matter with him. — *hu ká shú ngún nung gó.*

He has fever and dysentry. — *hu du dak sa luk-má múng zak.*

Give him some medicine, he will recover. — *hum món tyám byi, hu hrók sho.*

I am helpless, there is no remedy, he will die. — *go bóng ma lyek ne, thya ma nyin ne hu mák sho.*

You must contrive to do something to enable him to recover, nurse him well.

hó nun hum sa la mát shang, sa-re la thám-jú mát gát, hum ryú la dak. [zúk sho.

I shall do all in my power.

go, sa-re khu tet,

I am happy to hear it.

go, thyo wung sa, sák-di ma.

It has become night, it is dangerous in the hills groping about in the dark.

so-náp nón ne, rók ká tyáng ká thap yáp la nóng ngung, rom lyáng gum.

You have no torch, we will wait here till the light of dawn.

bók-zu ma nyin ne, á-bá so-óm tet bám sho.

Can you read and write?

hó rok pi ya wung a.

I can do neither, no one ever taught me.

nyum la ma thyák ne, to la hláp ma bo ne.

Induce your elders to teach you, exert yourself also to learn.

ran bo sang hláp bo shang thyeng nga, hó-do sa la ko shang nyer la mát ta.

Whose land is this?

á-re to sa fat nyi a.

It belongs to the state, it is common property; it was confiscated by Government.

tem-bo sa nyi, á-der gum, júng je nón.

What amount of wheat and barley do you get for the rupee? — *kóm kát ká ka-cher sa kyo sóng sa-tet thop shang a.*

You will obtain about eighty lbs. — *fri* (a measure of about 8 lbs.) *ka-ti tshet rup sho.*

When will we reach our resting place? — *gór lyáng sa-thá khya sho.*

Can you see the tents? — *kúr pang shim khu a.*

We will arrive presently. — *á-nye thi sho.*

There is a poor man, give him some charity. — *ma-ró jan kyong bo nyi, hum jum-bo tóng.*

Let no opportunity of doing good escape, emulate each other in virtue and purity, be humble, pray to God and trust in Him; farewell. — *á-ryúm mát shang ká jo-tshóng ma lyót tun, kát nun kát ká kum-yo kum-bá tung-gli tung-sóng ká gyan na le, á-yú-dom nyom-chhúng mát ta, rum ká ma lung tát byi; ryú la bám ma o.*

END OF GRAMMAR.